Easy
Chinese
Cookbook

SPRING ROLLS, PAGE 26

Easy Chinese Cookbook

Restaurant Favorites Made Simple

Chris Toy

ROCKRIDGE
PRESS

For general information on our other products and services or to obtain technical support, please contact our Customer Care Department within the United States at (866) 744-2665, or outside the United States at (510) 253-0500.

Rockridge Press publishes its books in a variety of electronic and print formats. Some content that appears in print may not be available in electronic books, and vice versa.

Interior and Cover Designer: Michael Patti
Art Producer: Sara Feinstein
Editor: Arturo Conde

Photography © 2020 Evi Abeler. All other art used under license from Shutterstock.com.

Food Styling by Albane Sharrard.
Author photo courtesy of © Kerry Michaels.

Title Page: Photography by Evi Abeler

ISBN: Print 978-1-64611-587-7 |
eBook 978-1-64611-588-4

R0

This book is in memory of
my parents, Alfred and Grace Toy,
who took me into their family—
the first baby adopted from
Hong Kong to the United States
in 1958 through the International
Social Service.

Contents

Introduction

SOME PEOPLE SAY THAT food can connect you with your origin. For me, Chinese food connects me with not only my birthplace—I was adopted from Hong Kong in 1958—but also my adoptive family, who ran Chinese restaurants in America.

My dad's family owned Toy's Chinese Restaurant in Milwaukee, Wisconsin, for over 90 years. My mom's side ran the King Joy Restaurant during the 1940s in Quincy, Massachusetts. And her brother and sister-in-law—James and Eleanor—have owned the Yangtze China Inn in West Bridgewater, Massachusetts, since the 1950s.

Today, Asian cuisine feeds my mind and heart because it makes me feel at home. Whether I'm on the road or at an important family gathering, the tastes and smells of my favorite dishes bring my family and friends closer and evoke powerful memories.

Ramen egg drop soup, for instance, reminds me of my dad; it was his favorite late-night snack, and we made it together after everyone else had gone to bed. Although ramen noodles are Japanese, the word *ramen* comes from "lamian," the Chinese word for noodles. Chinese and Japanese cuisine share similar noodle soups with poached eggs, commonly known as egg drop soups.

Years later, I found myself re-creating that same dish on one burner in my college dorm room. After I got my own apartment, I started making wonton soup—the ultimate Chinese comfort food—to satisfy my appetite for home. Today, I share the same dish with my own children, just as my father did with me.

When I look back at Chinese American food, I also see layers of immigrant history that date back to the first Chinese migrants in the mid-1800s. The ingredients in each dish reveal exciting stories about where the migrants came from, how they preserved their culture, and how they adapted to mainstream America.

The Exciting (but Forgotten) Origin of Chinese Takeout Restaurants

The first Chinese immigrants arrived during the Gold Rush from the southeastern provinces of Guangdong (Canton) and Guangxi in 1849, seeking to mine their fortunes in the "golden mountains" of California. Later waves of migrants who also sought their fortunes affectionately called America "Meiguo," which literally means beautiful country. All of them yearned for authentic Chinese food that satisfied their nostalgia for family and home. This demand gave rise to restaurants and other establishments that served tasty, inexpensive, Cantonese-style food for homesick immigrants working on the railroad and in agriculture, as well as for hungry Americans.

Restaurants featuring Cantonese-style stir-fries with ginger, garlic, scallions, sliced meats, vegetables, and salty-sweet soy sauces became signature dishes in Chinese American cooking. For many Chinese restaurant families—including my parents, who emigrated from Canton—menus featured favorites like sweet and sour seafood, kung pao chicken, spareribs, and wonton soup.

Decades later, President Richard Nixon's 1972 visit to China sparked and renewed American interest in Chinese food. Televised diplomatic meals made Americans hungry for spicy pork and beef dishes made with peppers, shallots, ginger, and garlic from Sichuan; shrimp dumplings, steamed crab, and smoked fish slices from Shanghai; and the famous Peking duck from Beijing.

This book will help you re-create some of those historic dishes at home. And with each meal, you will be able to appreciate why Chinese Americans value food so much—sharing small dishes can bring family and friends close together, remind you of the people and places you love, and help you create new memories.

Re-creating Chinese American Food with Easy Recipes at Home

While Chinese home cooking can feel challenging and intimidating, these recipes are both seriously easy and cheap. Not long ago, you had to find a Chinatown in the heart of a big city to get fresh, authentic ingredients. But that taste of Chinatown is now widely available online and at local stores, where popular Chinese ingredients like scallions, garlic, soy sauce, and wrappers are sold.

This cookbook offers over 85 recipes to help you re-create classic Chinese takeout dishes at home. In addition to tasting great, these recipes will add healthy ingredients like fresh ginger and garlic to your diet, and they will help you stay on budget—the average American spends as much money on groceries as they do on takeout and dining out combined!

CHAPTER ONE

THE CHINESE HOME KITCHEN

When I remember my family's kitchens—at home and in the restaurant—there was always a Chinese cleaver and a heavy-duty cutting board. The cleaver's large blade sliced, diced, flattened, scooped, tenderized, and ground ingredients into flavorful dishes.

The kitchens were also equipped with curved iron woks—black, well oiled, and ready to be heated to high temperatures that released the pungent aromas of fresh ginger, garlic, and scallions. This chapter brings you into the heart of an authentic Chinese kitchen and introduces the tools, techniques, and ingredients needed to re-create your favorite takeout dishes at home.

Unlocking the Flavors of China

Flavor bases are combinations of ingredients that give food a distinct taste and smell that is characteristic of a region, culture, and climate. In Chinese cooking, these ingredients include aromatic vegetables and herbs or spices that are cooked in oil or butter.

China is a vast country with a long tradition of strong regional cuisines. And even though these regions give Chinese food a wide range of contrasting flavors, the most popular takeout recipes start off with similar bases. Many of the recipes in this book rely on what Americans often consider to be the heart of Chinese American cooking: the Cantonese base. Some recipes use the spicier Sichuan and Hunan bases.

THE CANTONESE BASE

Chinese American dishes were heavily influenced by Cantonese-style cooking until the 1970s. Baby boomers grew up ordering shrimp fried rice, egg rolls, and kung pao chicken from local menus. They made takeout—ordering food to be eaten at home—a fixture in Chinese American restaurants. And these fast, cheap dishes became the favorite comfort foods for many families.

Growing up, my family's favorite dishes were also Cantonese-based. Like many Chinese Americans, we enjoyed chicken lo mein, beef with broccoli, and wonton soup. These favorites are prepared with the Cantonese flavor base: ginger, garlic, and scallions.

Cantonese base ingredients are used in different combinations and in a variety of ways throughout this cookbook. My Sweet and Sour Chicken (see page 49) and Wonton Soup (see page 36) both list them as base ingredients. But although the chicken recipe lightly browns crushed ginger and garlic in hot oil for flavor, the soup recipe incorporates the garlic and ginger into the filling after chopping and mixing them with a cleaver. The flavors are released into the soup as the wontons boil.

MY FAVORITE CANTONESE DISH

One of my favorite Cantonese dishes is Whole Fried Fish (see page 82). My family ordered it at special banquets and made it at home for Chinese New Year. In Chinese culture, the fish is a symbol of togetherness, good fortune, and abundance. This dish is usually eaten with family and friends, and the head of the fish is served facing the head of the family or a guest of honor. The perfect fried fish is cooked to the bone and moist. Chinese tradition says the diner who eats one of the fish eyes will have good fortune for seven years!

THE SICHUAN AND HUNAN BASES

America was first introduced to the hot and spicy dishes of Sichuan and Hunan cuisine in 1972, during President Nixon's historic visit to China. The nationally televised state dinners triggered a new Chinese restaurant boom.

Like the Cantonese base, these flavor bases start with ginger, garlic, and scallions. However, the Sichuan and Hunan bases add peppercorns and hot chiles. Although similar, these flavor bases can vary from mild to hot. My General Tso's Chicken (see page 48), which hails from the Hunan province, uses fresh hot chiles, while my Sichuan Beef and Vegetables (see page 68) uses milder red pepper flakes and mouth-numbing ground Sichuan peppercorns.

Climate, geography, and local ingredients often shape the character and flavor of regional cuisines. The Sichuan Province is landlocked in Southwest China, and its warm but damp climate has made hot-spicy dishes popular. For generations, many people in this region added generous amounts of ground Sichuan peppercorns, dried chiles, black beans, garlic sauce, rice wine, and hot sesame oil to create signature comfort foods that relieve overpowering humidity.

Similarly, the Hunan Province is landlocked in South-Central China on the banks of one of the longest rivers in the world: the Yangtze. This gives the region's climate and geography much variety, and you can taste it in dishes that combine hot chiles with scallions, honey, and hoisin sauce, such as my Cold Spicy Peanut Sesame Noodles (see page 109).

MY FAVORITE HUNAN DISH

Not all Hunan dishes are hot and spicy. One of my favorites is my Red Cooked Pork (*Hong Shao Rou*, see page 60), which is savory and sweet. As in many barbecue pork recipes, this is a melt-in-your-mouth dish. On my first trip to the Great Wall of China, the host of a small banquet told me that this dish was also the favorite of Chairman Mao!

THE TONGUE-TINGLING SICHUAN PEPPERCORN

Did you know that when you eat signature Sichuan dishes, you taste some spiciness followed by a tingling, numbing sensation in and around your mouth? This is caused by Sichuan peppercorns—the dried, roasted berries that are picked from prickly ash trees. Scientists say that the chemical hydroxy-alpha-sanshool in these tiny fruits stimulates tactile sensors in our mouths. It's similar to capsaicin in chiles, which makes our mouths feel like they're burning. My Sichuan Chicken (see page 53) and Mapo Ground Pork and Tofu (see page 63) will satisfy your palate for spiciness. If you prefer something milder, try my Hot and Sour Soup (see page 39).

The Chinese Pantry

The typical Chinese pantry may have dozens of ingredients, reflecting China's vast geography and climate—from the wet tropical south, to the temperate oceans in the east, to the dry inland deserts, to the cold rugged mountains farther west. However, this cookbook focuses on accessible ingredients. Almost everything listed on pages 4 to 8 can be found at your local grocery store. If it's not there, try finding it at an Asian market, a farmers' market, or online (see Resources on page 136). Common ingredients in many Chinese American pantries today have been passed down as part of a long immigrant legacy that shows how families adapted to the popular ingredients of the United States while remaining authentic to the taste of their Chinese origin.

ESSENTIAL SPICES

▪ **Chinese five-spice powder:** This spice mix is made up of ground Sichuan peppercorns, star anise, cloves, cinnamon, and fennel seeds. If you have a spice or coffee grinder, you can grind your own.

- **Garlic:** This is a bulb in the same family as onions and leeks. Find it in the produce department of your local grocery store. Farmers' markets sell garlic in early summer. Garlic is native to China and, along with ginger, it is a key component in all Chinese flavor bases.

- **Ginger:** Ginger is often crushed with garlic to flavor oil for stir-frying. Note that when crushing and chopping ginger with garlic, there's no need to remove the skin. A 1-by-1-inch piece of ginger makes about 1 tablespoon of grated ginger. Extra ginger can be frozen and grated as needed. Once frozen, it can't be thawed as it will be soggy.

- **Ground white pepper:** This is hotter than black pepper but less complex in taste. Ground white pepper adds heat and flavor to soups and stir-fries.

- **Red pepper flakes:** The heat from these dried hot chiles will make your dishes stand out when combined with ground Sichuan peppercorns and other ingredients. Chiles are a key ingredient in the Sichuan and Hunan flavor bases.

- **Sichuan peppercorns:** Contrary to its name, this is a tiny fruit with a mild citrus flavor that is picked from prickly ash trees. They can be used whole or ground. It is simpler to buy ground peppercorns; grinding at home requires sorting out the seeds from the husks. If you grind the seeds, the dish will be gritty. Ground Sichuan peppercorns give a tingling numbness to your tongue and mouth.

SAUCES, WINES, AND CONDIMENTS

- **Black bean paste:** This paste is made from fermented black beans, chiles, and garlic. It is a strongly pungent rub used for roasting meats but not as a dip or condiment.

- **Black vinegar:** This vinegar is fermented from charred brown rice. It is stronger than balsamic vinegar and not so sweet. Black vinegar pairs well with soy sauce or spicy sesame oil as a dip. It is a key ingredient in my Hot and Sour Soup (see page 39).

- **Chinese cooking wine:** This cooking wine is fermented from rice. As a marinade, it flavors and tenderizes meats for roasting or stir-frying. It is dry with hints of acidity and spice. The most popular brand of Chinese cooking wine is Xiaoxing.

- **Hoisin sauce:** This is a mix of fermented soybean paste, fennel, peppers, vinegar, and garlic. It glazes meats and is used as a sauce in stir-fries. It pairs with soy sauce or vinegar as a dipping sauce.

- **Hot sesame oil:** This gives recipes the nuttiness of toasted sesame and the heat of chiles. With a low smoke point, it cannot be used for stir-frying. Sesame oil works well in marinades, dipping sauces, or drizzled over a dish before serving.

- **Oyster sauce:** This sauce was created by accident when the founder of the Lee Kum Kee sauce company overcooked a pot of simmering oysters. Hours later, it had cooked into a dark, savory sauce.

- **Soy sauce:** This sauce is made by fermenting soybeans with salt brine and wheat. Gluten-free soy sauce is made using rice.

WHAT'S THE DEAL WITH MSG?

Perhaps one of the most controversial acronyms in the culinary world, MSG—short for monosodium glutamate—is negatively linked with Chinese food in America. It was created in 1908 by Japanese chemist Kikunae Ikeda, who discovered that isolating the amino acid glutamate—naturally occurring in mushrooms, tomatoes, and cheese—enhances the savory flavor of food. Starting in the 1930s, MSG became a key ingredient in many canned American soups. Patrons of Chinese takeout after World War II ate large quantities of MSG from canned and frozen foods at those restaurants.

Growing concerns about pesticides, chemicals, and food additives in the 1960s labeled MSG as the source of "Chinese restaurant syndrome," which was said to cause headaches, irregular heartbeat, rashes, and other ailments. While the US Food and Drug Administration (FDA) and other government organizations failed to conclude that MSG causes adverse effects and even deemed it safe, some individuals may be sensitive, and their dietary preferences and restrictions should be respected.

MSG still stirs up much controversy, but it is also reemerging as a food trend. Regardless, this book does not recommend using MSG. All of these recipes follow one basic principle: A balanced, well-prepared meal has all the nutrition and flavor that you want and need.

DRIED GOODS

- **Chow fun noodles:** These are wide, flat rice noodles that originated in the Guangzhou Province.

- **Dried lily buds:** These are the unopened buds of the common daylily. They are used in stir-fries as well as my Hot and Sour Soup (see page 39). They represent wealth when eaten during Lunar New Year celebrations.

- **Dried shiitake mushrooms:** These add umami flavor and texture to recipes. While you can use fresh mushrooms, dried shiitakes have a meatier texture and more umami. Buy them sliced since they cost the same by weight.

- **Glutinous rice:** This is a special type of short-grain rice that is very starchy. It is also known as sweet rice or sticky rice.

- **Hong Kong noodles:** These are thin egg noodles that have been precooked. They are stir-fried, deep-fried, or baked to make chow mein.

- **Lapsang souchong:** This is a black tea from the Wuyi Mountains in the Fujian Province of south coastal China. Curing the tea leaves over smoky pine fires gives the tea a very strong smoky scent and taste. It is used to impart a rich smoky flavor to rice, tea eggs, and other dishes.

- **Lo mein noodles:** These are thick uncooked egg noodles. They are boiled for stir-fry recipes with a thick sauce like my Beef and Broccoli with Oyster Sauce (see page 66).

- **Long-grain white rice:** This is a type of rice served as a side dish in Chinese cooking. As rice grains get shorter, they become starchier and stickier. Medium- and short-grain rice are used for sushi and dessert rice.

VEGETABLES

- **Bok choy:** This is a cabbage in the mustard family. It has smooth white stalks with green leaves. Shanghai or baby bok choy is smaller with green spoon-shaped stalks and a milder flavor. Store it in open plastic bags in the crisper drawer.

- **Chinese broccoli (*Gai Lan*):** Chinese broccoli is more bitter than Western broccoli. Store it in an open bag in the crisper drawer.

- **Chinese eggplants:** Chinese eggplants are thinner than Western eggplants. Select a ripe Chinese eggplant with smooth skin. Press a finger against the skin. If it leaves an imprint, it is ripe. Store it in the crisper drawer.

- **Chinese yard-long beans:** These beans can grow up to 36 inches but are usually closer to 18 inches. Stir-fry them, as they tend to get soggy if boiled or steamed. Store long beans unwashed in an open bag in your crisper drawer.

- **Napa cabbage:** A cabbage in the mustard family, Napa cabbage forms an oblong light green head of crinkly leaves with wide, flat stems. Store it in an open plastic bag in the crisper drawer.

- **Scallions:** An important vegetable in Chinese cooking, scallions are combined with garlic and ginger in a signature flavor base. Use the green and white parts when called for in these recipes. Store them by placing their roots in a jar with an inch of water.

- **Snow peas:** These flat pea pods are consumed whole. In milder climates, they can grow in the winter, thus their name. The young shoots are used in stir-fries. Store snow peas unwashed in plastic bags in the crisper drawer.

The Equipment

Chinese kitchens have specialty equipment like woks and cleavers. These tools are recommended, but this book will focus only on the most essential equipment to deliver the best-tasting recipes. The book also offers easy workarounds that will give you similar results. Although you may find rare hidden treasures at garage sales and flea markets, prices and styles vary on equipment; remember that you get what you pay for. Read trusted reviews before buying and don't forget to trust your own hands-on experience—touching and using equipment is best. As always, buyer beware!

MUST-HAVES

- **Chinese cleavers:** These versatile tools do more than slice and dice. The blade's broad side crushes and the sharp edge chops ingredients like ginger and garlic (whenever you see the words *crushed and chopped* in an ingredients list, use this tool to do the work). The butt of the handle can grind and mash herbs and seeds like a mortar and pestle. Cleavers can press circles of dough for dumpling wrappers. Their width allows them to scoop ingredients into woks, soup pots, and bowls. Cleavers are rectangular, between 6 and 8 inches long, and made of carbon or stainless steel. Carbon steel is easier to sharpen, but it is susceptible to rust if it's not cared for properly. Stainless steel is beautiful, harder, and resists rusting, but it is more difficult to sharpen if it becomes dull. Expect to pay $50 to $125.

■ **Cutting boards:** These are important because most ingredients in Chinese cooking need to be cut before cooking. It's good to have two or three boards for meat, fish, and vegetables. Expect to pay $10 to $30.

■ **Honing steels:** These maintain the sharp edge on your cleaver. Sharp cleavers are safer for cutting; dull cleavers risk slipping and cutting you. Used before and after preparing food, the honing steel aligns microscopic teeth along the cutting edge without removing any metal, keeping your cleavers and knives sharp. Expect to pay $10 to $20.

■ **Woks:** The most versatile piece of equipment in the Chinese kitchen, woks stir-fry, roast, boil, steam, and deep-fry. Most Chinese kitchens have at least two woks. They nest together, store easily, and come in different sizes. Expect to pay $15 to $50.

NICE-TO-HAVES

■ **Automatic rice cooker:** It's not cheating! Rice cookers work with computer precision, automatically turning the heat down to cook the rice and signaling when it's done. There are rice cookers with settings for different types of rice, and some even play a little tune when the rice is done. Expect to pay $30 to $120.

■ **Colanders and strainers:** Available in a variety of sizes, these are good for draining noodles and washing the grit out of vegetables. I use a strainer with a handle as a pot insert when boiling bones and vegetable trimmings for soup, which allows for easy straining and leaves a nice savory broth behind. Expect to pay $10 to $20.

■ **Scoop strainers:** Saucer-shaped in various sizes, scoop strainers are used for skimming, straining, and deep-frying. They lift fish or egg rolls out of hot oil. They also strain noodles and wontons out of hot broth. Expect to pay $10 to $20.

- **Steamer baskets:** Turn the wok into a multilevel steamer with a steamer basket. They may be metal or bamboo, have open screened bottoms, and can be stacked several layers high. Steamers are common cooking and serving containers for traditional Chinese dim sum. Expect to pay $10 to $25.

- **Wok draining rack:** This rack sits on the rim of the wok, allowing you to drain and cool items that have been deep-fried. This item is very convenient and keeps the food warm and crispy. Expect to pay $10 to $15.

- **Wok scoops:** These are spatulas with a curved edge to fit the shape of the wok—great tools for stir-frying and serving. A long hollow or wooden handle will resist getting hot when used with oil or a hot wok. Expect to pay $10 to $20.

THE MAGIC OF THE WOK

The word *wok* means "cooking pot" in Chinese, but for many of us who grew up with this round-bottomed pot in the kitchen, it is also a lifeline for preserving, innovating, and re-creating our cuisine. For over two millennia, the wok has been used to stir-fry, roast, boil, steam, deep-fry, poach, panfry, sear, and braise the most irresistible Chinese dishes.

The wok's curved shape gives it an advantage over flat cookware—it distributes heat, avoids hot spots, and makes efficient use of your gas or electric stove. The inside curve helps you use less cooking oil and maintain high temperatures for stir-frying. As oil and juices move to the center, the hottest part of the wok, everything above and away keeps relatively cooler, reducing sticking and burning. Its round shape can cradle whole chickens and large cuts of meat, keeping marinades and juices close so they self-baste while roasting. Here are three important things to keep in mind before buying your first wok:

1. Seasoned carbon steel and cast iron woks are nonstick.
2. Teflon and other nonstick coatings cannot withstand stir-frying temperatures.
3. Stainless steel, aluminum, and copper do not lend themselves to being seasoned.

Follow these four simple steps to season a new or used wok:

1. Scrub it clean with soap and water.
2. Dry it completely.
3. Rub cooking oil on the inside and outside.
4. Place it upside down on a baking sheet and bake it for 30 minutes at 350°F.

Once seasoned, you will need to clean and maintain your wok differently from other cookware. Do not wash or scrub it with soap and water. Rinse it with warm water and use a scrubbing pad only if needed. Dry it on your stovetop. The wok will darken as layers of seasoning accumulate. You will know when your seasoned wok is preheated as soon as it starts to smoke.

Chinese Cooking Made Easy

Flavorful traditional recipes often require expensive cookware and uncommon ingredients that aren't practical. For example, it would be great to make wontons in a deep fryer, but it's not realistic for the average home cook to own one. In keeping with the welcoming spirit of Chinese cuisine, the recipes in this book are accessible to all readers, including workarounds for expensive cookware and substitutions for hard-to-find ingredients. These home-kitchen hacks will not only help you re-create and preserve the authenticity of Chinese takeout food but also make it easier to share more delicious dishes with family and friends.

HOW TO DEEP-FRY WITHOUT A DEEP-FRYER

Many Chinese cooks will tell you that deep-frying is second only to stir-frying. Popular takeout recipes like egg rolls, spring rolls, wontons, and crab Rangoon are all deep-fried. Here are some effective workarounds if you don't have a deep-fryer.

Your best workaround is using a wok. A round-bottomed wok with a cradle is best, but you can also use a flat-bottomed one. If you have a wok draining rack (see page 10), use it for deep-frying. Follow these practical steps:

1. Pour 2 inches of oil into the wok.

2. Heat the oil to 350°F or until a wooden chopstick bubbles when placed in the oil.

3. Test fry one item. Cook it until it's lightly browned.

4. Remove the item with tongs or a skimmer. (Remember that whatever you put in the wok will cool down the oil. So don't overload it.)

If you don't have a wok, then the next best workaround is a Dutch oven. A deep cast iron skillet (5 to 6 inches) can also work. Make sure you have enough oil to cover whatever you're frying but also enough headspace so the oil doesn't overflow when you put the food in. Set a wire rack with paper towels nearby to drain and cool deep-fried food.

HOW TO STIR-FRY WITHOUT A WOK

Many favorite takeout recipes, including Kung Pao Beef (see page 70), Sichuan Chicken (see page 53), and fried rice, require stir-frying. While a wok is best for these dishes, you can use substitutes to get good results.

The best workaround for stir-frying without a wok is a large, well-seasoned heavy cast iron skillet. You want it to be heavy so the heat is evenly distributed, and it can remain hot for when more ingredients are added. If you use a stainless steel skillet, it needs to be large so that you can stir ingredients without crowding them or pushing them out of the pan. Nonstick skillets are not good because they are not heavy enough, and the nonstick coating can't hold up to the high temperatures for stir-frying. Follow these practical steps to stir-fry in your skillet:

1. Preheat the skillet and put 3 to 4 tablespoons of oil in the pan (you'll need more oil because of the flat surface).

2. Proceed as with regular stir-fry but cook in smaller batches (the flat skillet won't provide the curved shape of the wok for holding the ingredients in the pan close to the heat).

HOW TO STEAM RICE WITHOUT A RICE COOKER

An automatic rice cooker can make life easier, but it's possible to make perfectly good rice without one. This recipe was passed down to me from my mother. It's a reliable workaround for cooking rice without a rice cooker. Here are five simple steps:

1. Keep in mind that uncooked rice doubles in size after it cooks. If you want ½ cup of cooked rice, use ¼ cup of uncooked rice, scaling up as needed.

2. Place the rice in a heavy pot that is more than twice the volume of the uncooked rice. This gives the rice enough space to expand and will minimize boiling over.

3. Add enough water so that when you touch the top of the rice with the tip of your index finger, the water covers the first joint or up to the first line on the inside of your finger.

4. Cover the rice and bring it to a boil. As soon as you hear the water boiling or see steam escaping from beneath the cover, turn the heat down to its lowest setting.

5. Let the rice cook on low for 15 minutes. Do not lift the cover before then. When you lift the lid, steam escapes and the pressure drops. This causes the temperature to drop, and while the outside of your rice continues to cook and become mushy, the inside will remain uncooked.

These instructions are for white rice. Cook brown rice, covered, for twice as long (30 minutes).

Tips and Labels

For many of the recipes in this book, I have included some tips for shortcuts, substitutions, cooking techniques, and heat regulation. While I want you to benefit from my suggestions, I encourage you to experiment and make these recipes your own.

- **Substitution Tips:** These provide you with alternative ingredients that will give you results similar to those in the written recipe, just in case you don't have the indicated ingredients on hand.

- **Take a Shortcut:** These are suggestions for shortening the total amount of time it takes to prepare a recipe while achieving similar results as in the written recipe.

- **Troubleshooting:** These tips provide you with advice for ensuring the best results while preparing the recipe.

- **Heat Check:** These are suggestions for regulating the level of spiciness in your recipe.

You'll also see one of the following four labels near the top of each recipe. These are intended to indicate whether the dish is quick to make or follows certain dietary restrictions:

- 30 Minutes or Less
- Soy-Free
- Gluten-Free
- Vegetarian

Just a note regarding any dietary restrictions, especially if you have severe allergies (e.g., gluten intolerance) that involve personal health and safety. Please be sure to read the ingredient labels of commercially prepared sauces and other ingredients to ensure they do not contain allergens and have not been processed in facilities that have been in contact with allergens.

The Virtues of a Chinese Meal

The traditional Chinese greeting is "*Chi le ma?*" in Mandarin and "*Sik fan ma?*" in Cantonese, which literally translates to "Have you eaten today?" Growing up Chinese American, family and food were always strongly connected. My earliest memories are of eating breakfast with my parents and younger sister. Every morning we started our day with one of my favorite dishes—sweet and savory jook, which is a Cantonese porridge made of leftovers.

Looking back, jook shows me that inside every meal—how we make it, when we eat it, and who we eat it with—are larger community and family values that get passed down from generation to generation. This particular meal makes it clear to me that all values, like slow-cooked recipes, take time, effort, and care to grow. My mom would start making jook the night before by adding water, bits of leftovers, and bones into the leftover rice; then, she'd let it simmer until bedtime.

Family and food are still very present in my life. And when I think about important family meals during holidays, birthdays, graduations, weddings, and funerals, I am reminded that food brings people closer and compels them to sit together, share dishes, and create new memories.

Chinese culture is focused on family, and food for me is very much about celebrating that. By contrast, eating alone is like eating to survive—to simply stay alive. And in a way, this cookbook should also be understood as a guide to find sustenance beyond nutrition. It aims to feed the spirits of your family and friends not just from time to time but regularly as an important tradition.

Whether you share one meal daily with family (like I did growing up) or gather together with friends once a week, the values passed down through these Chinese dishes will remind you that food is one of the most meaningful ways we connect with one another.

Chinese people sometimes say that the most important thing you can do for another person is feed them. My wish is that you will use these recipes to bring everyone you love closer together. I hope you create new food experiences that strengthen your family, friends, and community.

POT STICKERS (GUOTIE), **PAGE 22**

CHAPTER TWO

DUMPLINGS, EGG ROLLS, AND OTHER APPETIZERS

This chapter provides a sampling of recipes traditionally eaten at or near the beginning of Chinese meals in restaurants, from takeout menus, or at home.

Boiled Dumplings *(Jiaozi)*

MAKES 4 DOZEN DUMPLINGS / PREP TIME: 30 MINUTES / COOK TIME: 5 MINUTES

Jiaozi are a traditional Chinese New Year food and popular in traditional Chinese dim sum. Serve them with a salty, spicy, or sour dipping sauce.

---

2 tablespoons crushed and chopped fresh ginger

4 garlic cloves, crushed and chopped

½ pound ground pork

1 cup chopped Napa cabbage

1 bunch (6 to 8) scallions, finely chopped

½ cup soy sauce, divided

2 tablespoons black vinegar

1 teaspoon hot sesame oil

1 package round wonton wrappers

2 quarts salted water

1. Use a Chinese cleaver or chef's knife to chop together the ginger, garlic, pork, cabbage, scallions, and ¼ cup of soy sauce.

2. In a small bowl, whisk together the remaining ¼ cup of soy sauce with the black vinegar and sesame oil. Set aside.

3. Fill a small bowl with water. Place 1 teaspoon of filling horizontally on the center of a wonton wrapper in the shape of a football. With two fingers, paint the perimeter of the wrapper with water from the bowl. Fold the wrapper in half to enclose the filling and form a half-moon shape, pressing firmly along the perimeter to remove excess air and seal the dumpling. Repeat this process with the remaining filling and wrappers.

4. Bring the salted water to a boil over medium-high heat. Add the dumplings and cook for 2 to 3 minutes, until the dumplings float and the wrapper is translucent. Drain the dumplings and serve with the dipping sauce.

TROUBLESHOOTING: Avoid overfilling the wrapper. If the filling gets on the edges of the wrapper, the dumpling won't seal.

MAKE YOUR OWN DUMPLING WRAPPERS

Most grocers carry 3-inch wonton wrappers and 6-inch egg roll wrappers. Some carry round wrappers for jiaozi or pot stickers, but you can always make your own, too.

Dumpling Wrappers

**MAKES 24 (3-INCH) WRAPPERS /
PREP TIME: 1 HOUR**

Using hot water is important: It helps the gluten in the dough form more quickly, making the dough soft and stretchy sooner.

2 cups all-purpose flour, plus more for dusting

¾ cup hot tap water

1 teaspoon kosher salt

1. Combine the flour, water, and salt in a medium bowl and knead until a soft ball of dough forms.

2. Generously dust a clean work surface with flour, then turn out the dough and knead it for 10 to 15 minutes, until the dough is smooth and elastic. Lightly dust the dough with flour as needed if it sticks to your hands.

3. Form the dough into a ball. Dust it with flour and place it in a zip-top bag. Let it rest for 30 minutes.

4. Turn out the dough and knead it a second time for 5 minutes, until it is very smooth, soft, and elastic.

5. Form the dough into a donut-shaped ring about 1 inch thick. Cut the ring to form a dough rope. Cut the dough rope into 24 uniform pieces by repeatedly cutting the rope in half.

6. Roll out each piece of dough into a 3-inch circle. Roll out no more than 6 wrappers at a time to prevent them from drying out too quickly as you prepare the dumplings.

TAKE A SHORTCUT: Use a food processor fitted with a metal blade instead of kneading by hand. Process for 5 minutes, or until the dough forms a shaggy ball.

TROUBLESHOOTING: Dust unused dough or wrappers with flour and store them in a zip-top bag in the refrigerator or freezer. Allow them to return to room temperature before use.

Fried Wontons

MAKES 4 DOZEN WONTONS / PREP TIME: 30 MINUTES / COOK TIME: 10 MINUTES

These deep-fried, flavorful dumplings are great for parties. They can be heated up in a 300°F oven for 10 minutes. Experiment with different fillings, such as chopped vegetables and tofu or chopped fruit and warming spices.

¾ pound ground pork

3 garlic cloves, crushed and chopped

2 tablespoons soy sauce

1 tablespoon crushed and chopped fresh ginger

1 package square wonton wrappers

Vegetable oil, for frying

Sweet and Sour Duck Sauce (see page 123), for serving

1. Use a Chinese cleaver or chef's knife to chop together the pork, garlic, soy sauce, and ginger.

2. Fill a small bowl with water. Place a wonton wrapper down so it looks like a baseball diamond with you sitting behind home plate. Place ½ teaspoon of filling on the pitcher's mound. With two fingers, paint the perimeter baselines with water from the bowl. Fold the wrapper in half, connecting home plate with second base to enclose the filling and form a triangle shape. Press firmly along the perimeter to remove excess air and seal the dumpling. Repeat this process with the remaining filling and wrappers.

3. In a wok or Dutch oven, heat 1 inch of oil to 350°F, or until a wooden chopstick bubbles when placed in the oil.

4. Place wontons, a few at a time, into the oil, and cook for 10 to 15 seconds, turning once, or until evenly golden brown.

5. Serve immediately with the duck sauce for dipping.

TROUBLESHOOTING: Be sure the perimeter of the wonton wrapper is painted with water to ensure a good seal.

Crab Rangoon

MAKES 4 DOZEN CRAB RANGOON / PREP TIME: 30 MINUTES / COOK TIME: 10 MINUTES

Although this isn't actually Chinese or even Asian in origin, it is very popular as an appetizer in Chinese restaurants. The key ingredient, cream cheese, is non-existent in Asian cuisine. The dish can be served hot or cold.

---

1 (8-ounce) package picked crabmeat

1 (8-ounce) package plain or flavored cream cheese

3 garlic cloves, crushed and chopped

1 teaspoon soy sauce

1 package square wonton wrappers

Vegetable or peanut oil, for frying

Sweet and Sour Duck Sauce (see page 123), for serving

1. Use a Chinese cleaver or chef's knife to chop together the crabmeat, cream cheese, garlic, and soy sauce.

2. Fill a small bowl with water. Place a wonton wrapper down so it looks like a baseball diamond with you sitting behind home plate. Place 1 teaspoon of filling on the pitcher's mound. With two fingers, paint the perimeter baselines with water from the bowl. Fold each of the bases toward the pitcher's mound to enclose the filling and form a square shape. Pinch firmly along the seams to remove excess air and seal the dumpling. Repeat this process with the remaining filling and wrappers. Alternatively, pinch the center point of each baseline in toward the pitcher's mound to form a pinwheel.

3. In a wok or Dutch oven, heat 1 inch of oil to 350°F, or until a wooden chopstick bubbles when placed in the oil.

4. Place the dumplings, a few at a time, into the oil, and cook for 10 to 15 seconds, turning once, or until evenly golden brown.

5. Serve immediately with the duck sauce for dipping.

TROUBLESHOOTING: Let the wontons dry for 15 minutes or longer and press out excess air while folding to minimize expansion.

Pot Stickers *(Guotie)*

MAKES 4 DOZEN POT STICKERS / PREP TIME: 20 MINUTES / COOK TIME: 10 MINUTES

30 MINUTES OR LESS

It's said that these crispy, steamed dumplings were invented by a cook who accidentally burned the Emperor's steamed dumplings while chatting with the ladies of the court. The desperate cook poured water into the hot pan, replaced the cover, and created the Emperor's new favorite dish.

---

1 pound ground pork

5 scallions, chopped

4 ounces mushrooms, chopped

2 tablespoons crushed and chopped fresh ginger

3 garlic cloves, crushed and chopped

1 tablespoon hoisin sauce

1 package round wonton wrappers

Vegetable oil, for frying

2 tablespoons water

Soy and Vinegar Dipping Sauce (see page 121), for serving

1. Use a Chinese cleaver or chef's knife to chop together the pork, scallions, mushrooms, ginger, garlic, and hoisin sauce.

2. Fill a small bowl with water. Dip the perimeter of a wonton wrapper in a shallow bowl of water, wetting both sides around the edge.

3. Place 1 teaspoon of filling horizontally on the center of a wonton wrapper in the shape of a football. At the 12 o'clock (top center) position of the wrapper, make a pleat and flatten it. Repeat at the 1 o'clock, 2 o'clock, 11 o'clock, and 10 o'clock positions to form an open pocket around the filling. Bring the edge of the 6 o'clock position up to the pleat at 12 o'clock and press to seal the edges together. Repeat this process with the remaining filling and wrappers.

4. Seal the dumplings by pressing all along the edges, then press down gently on the dumplings to form a flat base.

5. Cover the bottom of a skillet with oil and heat over medium-high heat to 300°F.

6. Place the dumplings in the oil, working in batches as necessary, and fry for 1 to 2 minutes, until the bottoms are golden brown. Then, partially cover the skillet, leaving ¼ inch of space, and pour in the water. Immediately cover the skillet completely to keep the steam inside and splattering oil to a minimum.

7. Steam the dumplings for 2 minutes. Lower the heat and lift the cover away from you so the steam and any oil are directed away from your face. Transfer the dumplings to a serving dish and repeat the process with the remaining dumplings.

8. Serve immediately with the dipping sauce.

TROUBLESHOOTING: You can fry the dumplings close together, but they shouldn't touch one another. Fry them in batches if necessary.

Egg Rolls

Egg rolls are larger and have a thicker shell than spring rolls. Some sources say that egg rolls were invented in the 1900s and were originally thin omelets wrapped around a filling of meat and vegetables.

---

2 tablespoons vegetable oil, plus more for deep frying

1 cup shredded carrots

3 garlic cloves, crushed and chopped

1 tablespoon crushed and chopped fresh ginger

1 pound ground pork

3 cups shredded Napa cabbage, shredded American cabbage, or store-bought coleslaw mix

1 bunch (6 to 8) scallions, chopped

1 package egg roll wrappers

Sweet and Sour Duck Sauce (see page 123), for serving

1. Heat the oil in a wok or large cast iron skillet over medium-high heat until the oil is just smoking. Add the carrots, garlic, and ginger and stir-fry for 1 minute. Add the ground pork and stir-fry for 2 minutes. Add the cabbage and scallions and stir-fry for 1 minute, then remove from the heat.

2. Drain any liquid from the filling mix or your egg rolls will get soggy and disintegrate while cooking.

3. Fill a small bowl with water. Place an egg roll wrapper down like a baseball diamond with you at home plate. Place 3 to 4 tablespoons of filling across the pitcher's mound in a horizontal cigar shape. With two fingers, paint the perimeter baselines with water from the bowl, paying special attention to second base. Bring first and third base together over the pitcher's mound and pinch together, overlapping no more than ¼ inch. Take home plate and tuck it up behind the pitcher's mound and roll the infield up toward second base. Be sure second base is well sealed by the wet wrapper. Repeat this process with the remaining filling and wrappers.

4. Meanwhile, in a wok or Dutch oven, heat 2 inches of oil to 350°F, or until a wooden chopstick bubbles when placed in the oil.

5. Place the egg rolls, 2 to 4 at a time, in the oil and fry, turning over when the edges brown, for 15 to 20 seconds per side, or until evenly golden brown. Repeat this process with the remaining egg rolls.

6. Serve immediately with the duck sauce.

TROUBLESHOOTING: Gently flatten each egg roll before deep-frying them so they're easier to turn over in the oil.

Spring Rolls

MAKES 20 SPRING ROLLS / PREP TIME: 20 MINUTES / COOK TIME: 10 MINUTES

30 MINUTES OR LESS, SOY-FREE, VEGETARIAN

Spring rolls are a tradition during Chinese New Year, which occurs in the spring. Spring roll wrappers do not contain egg—just water and flour—and they usually have vegetable fillings.

---

2 tablespoons vegetable oil, plus more for deep frying

1 cup shredded carrots

3 garlic cloves, crushed and chopped

1 tablespoon crushed and chopped fresh ginger

4 ounces mushrooms, chopped

3 cups finely shredded Napa cabbage or angel hair coleslaw

1 bunch (6 to 8) scallions, cut into ¼-inch pieces

1 package spring roll wrappers

Sweet and Sour Duck Sauce (see page 123), for serving

1. Heat the oil in a wok or large cast iron skillet over medium-high heat for about 2 minutes, until it shimmers. Add the carrots, garlic, and ginger and stir-fry for 1 minute. Add the mushrooms and stir-fry for 1 minute. Add the cabbage and stir-fry for 1 minute. Remove the wok from the heat and stir in the scallions.

2. Fill a small bowl with water. Place a spring roll wrapper down like a baseball diamond with you at home plate. Place 2 tablespoons of filling across the pitcher's mound in a horizontal cigar shape. With two fingers, paint the perimeter baselines with water from the bowl, paying special attention to second base. Bring first and third base together over the pitcher's mound and pinch together, overlapping no more than ½ inch. Take home plate and tuck it up behind the pitcher's mound and roll the infield up toward second base. Be sure second base is well sealed by the wet wrapper. Repeat this process with the remaining filling and wrappers.

3. Meanwhile, in a wok or Dutch oven, heat 2 inches of oil to 350°F, or until a wooden chopstick bubbles when placed in the oil.

4. Place the spring rolls, 2 to 4 at a time, in the oil and fry, turning over when the edges brown, for 10 to 15 seconds per side, or until evenly golden brown. Repeat this process with the remaining spring rolls.

5. Serve immediately with the duck sauce for dipping.

TROUBLESHOOTING: Make sure that the "second base" corner is well moistened so it doesn't open up while frying.

Fish Balls

MAKES 16 FISH BALLS / PREP TIME: 20 MINUTES / COOK TIME: 10 MINUTES

30 MINUTES OR LESS

Fish balls are a classic Chinese street food. The secret to light and bouncy fish balls is chopping and mixing the fish until it is a very smooth paste. The longer it's mixed, the lighter and bouncier the balls will be. Serve as appetizers or use as dumplings in soup.

---

1 pound whitefish, such as tilapia, cod, or haddock

2 tablespoons rice wine

1 teaspoon kosher salt

1 teaspoon toasted sesame oil

½ teaspoon ground white pepper

2 to 3 quarts salted water

Soy and Vinegar Dipping Sauce (see page 121), for serving

1. Use a Chinese cleaver or chef's knife to chop together the fish, rice wine, salt, sesame oil, and white pepper for 10 minutes to form a smooth paste.

2. Fill a large bowl with ice water and a small bowl with tap water. Wet your hands with water from the small bowl and pinch enough fish paste to form ½-inch fish balls by rolling them gently between your palms. Place the fish balls in the large bowl of ice water until ready to cook. Wet your hands as necessary to reduce sticking.

3. Bring the salted water to a boil in a pot over medium-high heat. Add the fish balls and cook for 3 to 4 minutes, until they float.

4. Serve immediately with the dipping sauce.

TAKE A SHORTCUT: Use a food processor with a metal blade to process the ingredients for 2 to 3 minutes instead of chopping by hand in step 1.

Satay Chicken Skewers

SERVES 2 TO 4 / PREP TIME: 10 MINUTES / COOK TIME: 10 MINUTES

30 MINUTES OR LESS

This peanut-based staple of Chinese takeout is actually from Indonesia. Although it is often made out of chicken breast, I prefer the darker and fattier thigh meat because it has more flavor.

---

4 tablespoons creamy peanut butter

3 garlic cloves, crushed and chopped

2 tablespoons soy sauce

1 tablespoon crushed and chopped fresh ginger

1 teaspoon hot sesame oil

1 pound boneless, skinless chicken thighs, cut lengthwise into 1-inch strips

Soy and Ketchup Dipping Sauce (see page 120), for serving

1. Set the broiler to high. If using wooden skewers, soak 6 to 8 of them in water for 15 minutes. You can also use metal skewers.

2. Meanwhile, in a medium bowl, whisk together the peanut butter, garlic, soy sauce, and sesame oil.

3. Seal the chicken and the marinade in a large zip-top bag. Massage for 2 minutes.

4. Thread the strips of marinated chicken onto the skewers with the thickest portion near the tip.

5. Broil the chicken directly under the broiler for 4 minutes per side, until the juices run clear when the chicken is pierced with a knife.

6. Serve immediately with the dipping sauce.

SUBSTITUTION TIP: Other meats such as beef, pork, and lamb can be substituted for chicken.

Sweet and Sour Chicken Wings

SERVES 2 TO 4 / PREP TIME: 5 MINUTES / COOK TIME: 40 MINUTES

It's been said that early Chinese restaurants made inexpensive chicken wings because the small wings were less desirable. They have come a long way. On Super Bowl Sunday, over 1.3 billion wings are consumed by viewers. These sweet, mildly spicy baked wings will definitely add to that total.

½ cup honey

¼ cup soy sauce

2 tablespoons rice or balsamic vinegar

2 tablespoons crushed and chopped fresh ginger

4 garlic cloves, crushed and chopped

1 tablespoon hot sesame oil

¼ cup cornstarch

3 pounds chicken wings

1. Preheat the oven to 350°F. Line a roasting pan just large enough to fit the wings in a single layer with aluminum foil.

2. In a medium bowl, whisk together the honey, soy sauce, vinegar, ginger, garlic, and sesame oil.

3. Seal the chicken with the marinade and cornstarch in a large zip-top bag. Massage for 2 minutes.

4. In the prepared roasting pan, place the wings in a single layer so they are just touching one another.

5. Roast for 40 minutes, turning once, or until the juices run clear when the chicken is pierced with a knife.

SUBSTITUTION TIP: You can substitute cider or red wine vinegar for the rice or balsamic vinegar.

Boneless Pork Appetizer *(Char Siu)*

**SERVES 2 TO 4 / PREP TIME: 10 MINUTES, PLUS OVERNIGHT
TO MARINATE / COOK TIME: 50 MINUTES**

Char siu means "fork roasted." Traditionally, strips of wild boar were marinated, skewered, and slow roasted over an open fire until caramelized. Today, we use pork shoulder (the fattier the better). Traditionally, the red color came from using a red fermented tofu, which is hard to find in the United States. Chinese restaurants and Chinatown meat shops use red food coloring.

½ cup honey

¼ cup brown sugar

2 tablespoons Chinese five-spice powder

1 tablespoon soy sauce

1 tablespoon toasted sesame oil

1 tablespoon hoisin sauce

4 garlic cloves, crushed and chopped

Few drops red food coloring (optional)

1 pound pork shoulder

1. Preheat the oven to 475°F. Add 1 inch of water to a roasting pan and place the roasting rack inside.

2. In a medium bowl, whisk together the honey, brown sugar, Chinese five-spice powder, soy sauce, sesame oil, hoisin sauce, garlic, and red food coloring (if using).

3. Seal the pork and marinade in a large zip-top bag. Massage for 2 minutes.

4. Transfer the marinated pork to the rack in the prepared roasting pan, reserving any marinade for basting. Roast for 50 minutes, turning the pork once and brushing with the marinade, or until an instant-read thermometer inserted into the thickest part of the meat registers 145°F.

5. Let the pork rest for 3 minutes, then slice against the grain and serve.

TROUBLESHOOTING: If you have time, you can lower the cooking temperature to 375°F and roast the pork for twice as long, turning it twice. This will make the pork more tender.

Sweet and Sour Spareribs

SERVES 2 TO 4 / PREP TIME: 10 MINUTES / COOK TIME: 1 HOUR

GLUTEN-FREE, SOY-FREE

This is one of my favorite appetizers. It can be cooked in as little as an hour, or you can lower the temperature to 250°F and slow cook it for twice as long for tender meat that almost falls off the bone. Ask a butcher to cut the ribs in half.

½ cup brown sugar

½ cup apple cider or balsamic vinegar

½ cup ketchup

1 tablespoon cornstarch

2 pounds baby back or St. Louis–style pork spareribs, cut into 2-inch pieces

1. Preheat the oven to 350°F.

2. In a medium bowl, whisk together the brown sugar, vinegar, ketchup, and cornstarch.

3. Place the ribs in a roasting pan large enough so that they are all touching and in a single layer (this will keep the marinade around the ribs, making them self-baste). Brush the ribs liberally with the marinade, reserving the rest for later.

4. Roast, uncovered, on the lower rack for 30 minutes. Brush the ribs with the marinade, turn them, and then brush them again. Roast for 30 minutes more, or until the meat is tender and almost falling off the bone.

5. Brush the ribs once more with the marinade, then serve.

TROUBLESHOOTING: Cuts of pork like this should reach a minimum internal temperature of 145°F. However, for very tender ribs, the target internal temperature is usually 190°F to 200°F.

Teriyaki Beef Skewers

SERVES 2 TO 4 / PREP TIME: 10 MINUTES / COOK TIME: 5 MINUTES

30 MINUTES OR LESS

Teriyaki originated in Japan. The word literally means "glazed and roasted." In Japan, teriyaki is usually made for fish dishes. Chinese takeout restaurants added ginger and garlic to the sauce and started using it with grilled meats such as beef and chicken.

¼ cup brown sugar

3 tablespoons rice wine

2 tablespoons soy sauce

3 garlic cloves, crushed and chopped

1 tablespoon crushed and chopped fresh ginger

1 pound boneless sirloin steak, cut into 1-inch strips

Soy and Ketchup Dipping Sauce (see page 120), for serving

1. Set the broiler to high. If using wooden skewers, soak 6 to 8 of them in water for 15 minutes. You can also use metal skewers.

2. Meanwhile, in a medium bowl, whisk together the brown sugar, rice wine, soy sauce, garlic, and ginger.

3. Seal the steak and marinade in a large zip-top bag. Massage for 2 minutes.

4. Thread the strips of marinated steak onto the skewers with the thickest portion near the tip.

5. Broil the steak directly under the broiler for 1 to 2 minutes, until your desired doneness is reached.

6. Serve immediately with the dipping sauce.

SUBSTITUTION TIP: Try this with thinly sliced marinated pork, chicken, or whole shrimp!

EGG DROP SOUP (*DANHUATANG*), PAGE 38

CHAPTER THREE

SOUPS AND SALADS

In traditional Chinese culture, soup is often considered to possess healing and medicinal benefits. Serve the soups in this chapter as main dishes or in smaller bowls as appetizers or sides. And yes, there are salads in Chinese cooking! The Chinese just don't refer to them as salads. They call them "cold food."

Wonton Soup

SERVES 4 TO 8 / PREP TIME: 20 MINUTES / COOK TIME: 5 MINUTES

30 MINUTES OR LESS, SOY-FREE

Wonton soup is the original Chinese comfort food. It was invented in the 1600s and originally reserved for the upper classes. When Chinese businessmen came to the United States to seek their fortunes, they brought it with them, and it became a staple of Chinese American takeout.

---

1 ounce sliced dried mushrooms

3 quarts half-strength chicken broth

3 garlic cloves, crushed and chopped

1 tablespoon crushed and chopped
  fresh ginger

¾ pound ground pork

1 package square wonton wrappers

2 cups chopped Napa cabbage

1 bunch (6 to 8) scallions, cut into
  ½-inch slices

1. In a Dutch oven or 4-quart pot over medium heat, combine the mushrooms and broth and let simmer while folding the wontons.

2. Use a Chinese cleaver or chef's knife to chop together the garlic, ginger, and ground pork.

3. Fill a small bowl with water. Place a wrapper down so it looks like a baseball diamond with you sitting behind home plate. Place ½ teaspoon of filling on the pitcher's mound. With two fingers, paint the perimeter baselines with water from the bowl. Fold the wrapper in half by bringing home plate up to second base to enclose the filling and form a triangle shape, pressing firmly along the perimeter to remove excess air and seal the dumpling. Repeat this process with the remaining filling and wrappers.

4. Increase the heat to high and bring the broth to a boil. (Note: Adding the wontons will lower the temperature, so getting the heat up to 212°F will maintain a quick cooking temperature.) Gently stir in the wontons, one or two at a time. Once they are all in the broth, cook for 2 minutes, then add the cabbage and cook for 1 minute.

5. Remove the soup from the heat and sprinkle the scallions on top, squeezing and bruising them to release more flavor.

6. Serve immediately.

TROUBLESHOOTING: Cook only as many wontons as you need. They are not good for leftovers because the wrappers fall apart. Freeze the uncooked wontons on baking sheets, then store them in zip-top bags in the freezer for up to a month.

Egg Drop Soup *(Danhuatang)*

SERVES 4 TO 8 / PREP TIME: 10 MINUTES / COOK TIME: 5 MINUTES

30 MINUTES OR LESS, GLUTEN-FREE, SOY-FREE, VEGETARIAN

In Chinese, the word *danhuatang* literally means "egg flower soup." To make this soup, eggs are slowly drizzled into boiling broth, forming billows of floating poached egg. Although some recipes call for poaching the egg whole, this one calls for beating the eggs before pouring them in.

---

8 cups vegetable broth, divided

½ teaspoon ground white pepper

2 tablespoons cornstarch

4 large eggs, beaten

4 scallions, finely chopped

1. In a Dutch oven or 4-quart pot over medium heat, combine 7 cups of broth and the white pepper and bring to a boil.

2. In a medium bowl, whisk together the cornstarch and the remaining 1 cup of broth, then stir the mixture into the broth for about 2 minutes, until it thickens.

3. Stir the broth clockwise for 10 seconds to get it moving together. While continuing to stir the broth in a clockwise motion, drizzle in the eggs, forming shreds.

4. Remove the soup from the heat and sprinkle in the scallions just before serving.

SUBSTITUTION TIP: Use chicken broth and add crumbled pork or shrimp and sliced vegetables after step 1 for a heartier, nonvegetarian meal.

Hot and Sour Soup

SERVES 4 TO 8 / PREP TIME: 20 MINUTES / COOK TIME: 5 MINUTES

30 MINUTES OR LESS, GLUTEN-FREE

A traditional Chinese New Year soup, this recipe combines the heat of hot sesame oil with the acidity of vinegar and the characteristic numbing effect of Sichuan peppercorns.

---

2 quarts plus 1 cup chicken broth, divided

¼ cup rice vinegar

1 teaspoon hot sesame oil

1 teaspoon ground Sichuan peppercorns

1 ounce sliced dried shiitake or tree ear mushrooms

12 dried lily buds

2 tablespoons cornstarch

½ pound ground pork

1 pound firm tofu, cut into ½-inch cubes

4 large eggs, beaten

1 bunch (6 to 8) scallions, cut into ¼-inch pieces

1. In a 4-quart pot over high heat, combine 2 quarts of the broth with the vinegar and sesame oil and bring to a boil. Stir in the peppercorns, dried mushrooms, and lily buds.

2. In a medium bowl, whisk together the cornstarch and the remaining 1 cup of broth, then stir the mixture into the broth for about 2 minutes, until it thickens.

3. Crumble the pork into the broth. Then, add the tofu.

4. While gently stirring the broth, drizzle in the eggs, forming shreds.

5. Remove the soup from the heat and sprinkle in the scallions just before serving.

SUBSTITUTION TIP: Substitute bamboo shoots for the lily buds if those are easier to find.

Cucumber Salad

SERVES 2 TO 4 / PREP TIME: 15 MINUTES

30 MINUTES OR LESS, VEGETARIAN

This is a perfect summer salad. The flavors of sweet, sour, and a little spice combined with the crunchy coolness of the cucumber is very refreshing.

---

1 English cucumber

3 garlic cloves, crushed and chopped

2 tablespoons rice vinegar

2 tablespoons soy sauce

2 tablespoons sugar

1 tablespoon toasted sesame oil

1 teaspoon hot sesame oil

Sesame seeds, for garnish

1. Cut the ends off the cucumber and score the cucumber skin all around with a fork. Cut the cucumber into 4-inch pieces.

2. Using the side of a Chinese cleaver or chef's knife, smash the cucumber pieces until they split open along their lengths. Remove and discard the seeds.

3. Cut the cucumber into bite-size cubes and place them in a bowl along with the cucumber juices.

4. Add the garlic, vinegar, soy sauce, sugar, and the toasted and hot sesame oils, tossing to mix well.

5. Garnish with sesame seeds and serve.

SUBSTITUTION TIP: Add fresh chopped herbs such as dill, cilantro, basil, or parsley as a garnish.

Grilled Napa Cabbage Salad

SERVES 2 TO 4 / PREP TIME: 10 MINUTES / COOK TIME: 5 MINUTES

30 MINUTES OR LESS, VEGETARIAN

This warm salad combines the caramelized sweetness of hoisin sauce and sesame oil with the slight mustard flavor of the Napa cabbage.

---

2 small or medium heads Napa cabbage

¼ cup hoisin sauce

2 tablespoons toasted sesame oil

1 tablespoon soy sauce

1 tablespoon rice, apple cider, or balsamic vinegar

1. Set the broiler to high.

2. Remove and discard any bruised or brownish stems from the cabbage. Halve (lengthwise) or quarter the cabbages.

3. In a medium bowl, whisk together the hoisin sauce, sesame oil, soy sauce, and vinegar. Brush half of the dressing on the flat side of each cabbage, reserving half of the dressing for later.

4. Transfer the cabbage, flat-side up, to a roasting pan or baking sheet and broil 3 inches away from the broiler element for 3 minutes, until lightly charred.

5. Brush the cabbage with the remaining half of the dressing and serve.

HEAT CHECK: For a bit of heat, you can substitute hot sesame oil for the toasted sesame oil.

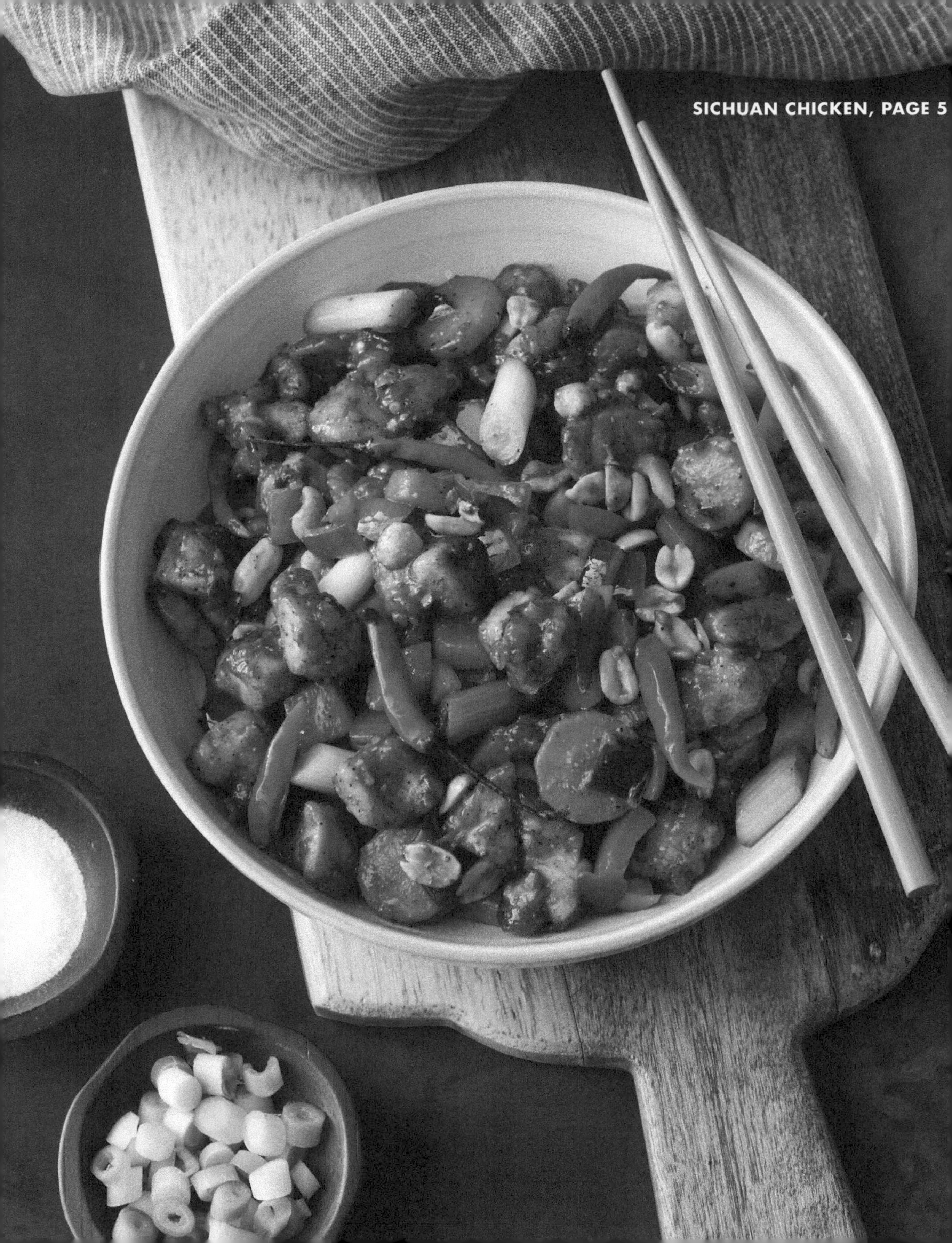
SICHUAN CHICKEN, PAGE 5

CHAPTER FOUR

POULTRY

According to archaeologists, chickens and ducks were domesticated for culinary purposes in China over 8,000 years ago. Just as in some Western cultures, soup made from chicken is thought to have medicinal healing powers. The recipes in this chapter will certainly help you feel good as you eat them!

Wok-Baked Whole Five-Spice Chicken

SERVES 4 TO 8 / PREP TIME: 10 MINUTES / COOK TIME: 1 HOUR 45 MINUTES

This is the only way I roast a whole chicken. The shape of the wok keeps the juices and marinade up against the breast as the chicken roasts upside down, which results in moist, tender meat.

¼ cup soy sauce

¼ cup brown sugar

3 tablespoons Chinese five-spice powder

2 tablespoons crushed and chopped fresh ginger

4 garlic cloves, crushed and chopped

1 (5- to 7-pound) chicken, whole, at room temperature

1. Preheat the oven to 375°F and adjust a rack to the lowest position.

2. In a medium bowl, whisk together the soy sauce, brown sugar, five-spice powder, ginger, and garlic, and then rub the mixture all over the chicken, being sure to get under the breast skin.

3. Place the chicken, breast-side down, in a wok or ovenproof bowl, and roast it on the lowest rack for 1 hour 15 minutes to 1 hour 45 minutes total, or until an instant-read thermometer inserted into the thickest part of the meat registers 165°F. When three-quarters of the total time has elapsed, turn the chicken breast up and roast it for the remainder of the time. The total cooking time will depend on the size of your bird; estimate 15 minutes per pound.

4. Remove the chicken from the oven and let it rest for 15 minutes, then serve.

HEAT CHECK: For a spicier flavor, add 2 tablespoons of hot sesame oil to the rub.

Cast Iron Roasted Chinese Chicken Thighs

SERVES 2 TO 4 / PREP TIME: 10 MINUTES / COOK TIME: 8 MINUTES

30 MINUTES OR LESS

This is a superfast and easy roasting method. My daughter Alex has loved it since she was a toddler, and I've always prepared it on her birthday. She still asks for her birthday chicken as an adult.

---

2 tablespoons vegetable oil, for greasing

1 pound boneless, skinless chicken thighs, at room temperature

2 tablespoons crushed and chopped fresh ginger

2 tablespoons soy sauce

2 tablespoons honey

2 tablespoons ketchup

3 garlic cloves, crushed and chopped

1. Grease a cast iron or oven-safe griddle or pan with the oil. Place the griddle 2 to 3 inches under the broiler element, set the broiler to high, and let the griddle heat for 10 minutes, or until it just begins to smoke.

2. Seal the chicken, ginger, soy sauce, honey, ketchup, and garlic in a large zip-top bag. Massage for 2 minutes.

3. Place the marinated chicken on the hot griddle and broil for 6 to 8 minutes, or until your desired doneness is reached. There's no need to flip the chicken because the hot cast iron will sear and cook it from the bottom.

4. Serve immediately.

SUBSTITUTION TIP: If you're using boneless chicken breasts, flatten them to a uniform ¼-inch thickness by covering them with plastic wrap and pounding them with a heavy object before marinating.

Moo Goo Gai Pan

SERVES 2 TO 4 / PREP TIME: 15 MINUTES / COOK TIME: 10 MINUTES

30 MINUTES OR LESS

In Chinese, the term *moo goo gai pan* literally translates to "mushrooms and sliced chicken." This Cantonese dish often includes other vegetables, but the umami of stir-fried mushrooms (moo goo) is what makes this a favorite for many.

1 tablespoon vegetable oil

3 garlic cloves, crushed and chopped

1 tablespoon crushed and chopped fresh ginger

1 pound boneless chicken thighs, cut into 1-inch pieces

4 ounces mushrooms, sliced

1 cup chopped bok choy (about ½-inch pieces)

2 tablespoons soy sauce

2 tablespoons oyster sauce

1 tablespoon cornstarch

1 bunch (6 to 8) scallions, cut into ½-inch pieces

Steamed rice (see page 12) or noodles, for serving

1. In a wok or large cast iron skillet, heat the vegetable oil over high heat for 2 minutes, or until it shimmers. Add the garlic and ginger and cook for about 1 minute, until lightly browned.

2. Add the chicken and stir-fry for 2 minutes. Add the mushrooms and stir-fry for 2 minutes. Add the bok choy and stir-fry for 1 minute.

3. In a medium bowl, whisk together the soy sauce, oyster sauce, and cornstarch, then stir the mixture into the wok to form a glaze.

4. Garnish with the scallions and serve over steamed rice or noodles.

Lemon Chicken

SERVES 2 TO 4 / PREP TIME: 15 MINUTES / COOK TIME: 10 MINUTES

30 MINUTES OR LESS

This classic Chinese takeout stir-fry recipe uses the Cantonese flavor base. The lemon-based sweet and sour sauce gives it a light, refreshing taste.

½ cup chicken broth

¼ cup honey

Juice of 1 lemon (3 tablespoons)

3 garlic cloves, crushed and chopped

1 tablespoon crushed and sliced fresh ginger

1 tablespoon plus ¼ cup cornstarch, divided

1 pound chicken thighs, cut into 1-inch cubes

2 tablespoons soy sauce

1 tablespoon rice wine

½ cup vegetable oil

1 bunch (6 to 8) scallions, cut into 1-inch pieces

Steamed rice (see page 12), for serving

1. In a medium saucepan over medium-low heat, whisk together the broth, honey, lemon juice, garlic, ginger, and 1 tablespoon of cornstarch for about 2 minutes, until it thickens. Cover and set aside.

2. Seal the chicken, soy sauce, rice wine, and the remaining ¼ cup of cornstarch in a large zip-top bag. Massage for 2 minutes.

3. In a wok or large cast iron skillet, heat the oil over medium-high heat to 350°F, or until a wooden chopstick bubbles when placed in the oil.

4. Add the marinated chicken and fry for about 3 minutes, until golden brown. Transfer the chicken to a plate.

5. Remove and discard all the oil from the pan. Then, return the chicken to the pan and pour the warm sauce over the chicken, tossing to coat.

6. Garnish with the scallions and serve over steamed rice.

SUBSTITUTION TIP: Try substituting lime for the lemon for a different citrus flavor.

General Tso's Chicken

SERVES 2 TO 4 / PREP TIME: 10 MINUTES / COOK TIME: 10 MINUTES

30 MINUTES OR LESS

Although this popular recipe is named after an actual general who lived in the Hunan Province during the Qing dynasty, the people in his hometown and his relatives have said that they were unaware of the dish. A 2014 documentary called *The Search for General Tso* explores its origin.

¼ cup honey

2 tablespoons hoisin sauce

2 tablespoons crushed and chopped fresh ginger

2 tablespoons soy sauce

2 hot chiles, cut into ¼-inch pieces

3 garlic cloves, crushed and chopped

1 tablespoon rice vinegar

¼ cup plus 1 tablespoon cornstarch, divided

1 pound chicken thighs, cut into 1-inch cubes

1 teaspoon ground white pepper

½ cup vegetable oil

1 teaspoon sesame seeds

1 bunch (6 to 8) scallions, cut into ½-inch slices

Steamed rice (see page 12), for serving

1. Whisk together the honey, hoisin sauce, ginger, soy sauce, chiles, garlic, vinegar, and 1 tablespoon of cornstarch.

2. Seal the chicken, white pepper, and the remaining ¼ cup of cornstarch in a large zip-top bag. Massage for 2 minutes.

3. In a wok or large cast iron skillet, heat the oil over medium-high heat to 350°F, or until a wooden chopstick bubbles when placed in the oil.

4. Add the marinated chicken and fry for about 3 minutes, until golden brown. Transfer the chicken to a plate.

5. Remove and discard all but 2 tablespoons of oil from the pan. Add the sauce and cook over medium heat, stirring, for about 2 minutes, until it thickens. Add the chicken and toss to coat.

6. Garnish with the sesame seeds and scallions and serve over steamed rice.

HEAT CHECK: You can regulate the spiciness of this recipe by adjusting the chiles and white pepper. For more heat, add 1 teaspoon of hot sesame oil in step 1.

Sweet and Sour Chicken

SERVES 2 TO 4 / PREP TIME: 10 MINUTES / COOK TIME: 10 MINUTES

30 MINUTES OR LESS, GLUTEN-FREE, SOY-FREE

It's said sweet and sour chicken was brought to California from Southern China when early Chinese restaurants catered to immigrant and US gold miners and railroad workers. As workers made their way east, sweet and sour chicken moved with them.

---

1 pound chicken thighs, cut into 1-inch cubes

¼ cup cornstarch

½ cup vegetable oil

1 medium onion, diced into ½-inch pieces

2 tablespoons crushed and chopped fresh ginger

3 garlic cloves, crushed and chopped

1 red bell pepper, diced into ½-inch pieces

1 green bell pepper, diced into ½-inch pieces

1 cup pineapple chunks

½ cup brown sugar

¼ cup rice or apple cider vinegar

¼ cup ketchup

1 teaspoon sesame seeds

1 bunch (6 to 8) scallions, cut into ½-inch pieces

1. Seal the chicken and cornstarch in a large zip-top bag and shake to coat evenly.

2. In a wok or large cast iron skillet, heat the oil over medium-high heat to 350°F, or until a wooden chopstick bubbles when placed in the oil.

3. Add the coated chicken and fry for about 3 minutes, until golden brown. Transfer the chicken to a plate.

4. Remove and discard all but 1 tablespoon of oil from the pan. Add the onion, ginger, and garlic and stir-fry for 1 minute. Add the red and green bell peppers and pineapple and stir-fry for 1 minute.

5. Add the brown sugar, vinegar, and ketchup and stir until the sugar is dissolved and a sauce forms. Add the cooked chicken and stir to coat.

6. Garnish with the sesame seeds and scallions and serve.

SUBSTITUTION TIP: You can use balsamic or wine vinegar as a substitute for the rice and cider vinegar.

Orange Chicken

SERVES 2 TO 4 / PREP TIME: 10 MINUTES / COOK TIME: 10 MINUTES

30 MINUTES OR LESS

This favorite Chinese American takeout dish is adapted from an authentic Chinese recipe that uses dried orange peels for the citrus flavor. Here, we use fresh orange zest and juice.

---

1 pound chicken thighs, cut into 1-inch cubes

¼ cup plus 1 tablespoon cornstarch, divided

½ cup vegetable oil

3 garlic cloves, crushed and chopped

1 tablespoon crushed and chopped fresh ginger

1 cup freshly squeezed orange juice

Zest of 1 orange, grated

¼ cup brown sugar

2 tablespoons rice vinegar

1 tablespoon soy sauce

1 teaspoon hot sesame oil

1 teaspoon sesame seeds

1 bunch (6 to 8) scallions, cut into ½-inch pieces

Steamed rice (see page 12), for serving

1. Seal the chicken and ¼ cup of cornstarch in a large zip-top bag and shake to coat evenly.

2. In a wok or large cast iron skillet, heat the vegetable oil over medium-high heat to 350°F, or until a wooden chopstick bubbles when placed in the oil.

3. Add the coated chicken and fry for about 3 minutes, until golden brown. Transfer the chicken to a plate.

4. Remove and discard all but 2 tablespoons of vegetable oil from the pan. Add the garlic and ginger and stir-fry for about 1 minute, until lightly browned. Add the orange juice and zest, brown sugar, vinegar, soy sauce, sesame oil, and the remaining 1 tablespoon of cornstarch. Simmer and stir for about 2 minutes, until the sauce thickens. Add the chicken and stir to coat.

5. Garnish with the sesame seeds and scallions and serve over steamed rice.

SUBSTITUTION TIP: Try substituting lemon or lime zest for an interesting variation.

Sesame Chicken

SERVES 2 TO 4 / PREP TIME: 10 MINUTES / COOK TIME: 10 MINUTES

30 MINUTES OR LESS

This nutty, sweet stir-fry is a popular takeout item. Similar to my General Tso's Chicken (see page 48), it lacks the hot-spicy aspect. It's usually served simply with scallions, as it is in this recipe.

---

1 pound chicken thighs, cut into 1-inch cubes

¼ cup plus 1 tablespoon cornstarch, divided

½ cup vegetable oil

3 garlic cloves, crushed and chopped

1 tablespoon crushed and chopped fresh ginger

1 cup chicken broth

¼ cup brown sugar

2 tablespoons rice vinegar

2 tablespoons soy sauce

2 tablespoons rice wine

2 tablespoons toasted sesame oil

1 teaspoon sesame seeds

1 bunch (6 to 8) scallions, cut into ½-inch pieces

Steamed rice (see page 12), for serving

1. Seal the chicken and ¼ cup of cornstarch in a large zip-top bag and shake to coat evenly.

2. In a wok or large cast iron skillet, heat the vegetable oil over medium-high heat to 350°F, or until a wooden chopstick bubbles when placed in the oil.

3. Add the coated chicken and fry for about 3 minutes, until golden brown. Transfer the chicken to a plate.

4. Remove and discard all but 2 tablespoons of oil from the pan. Add the garlic and ginger and stir-fry for about 1 minute, until lightly browned. Add the chicken broth, brown sugar, vinegar, soy sauce, rice wine, sesame oil, and the remaining 1 tablespoon of cornstarch. Simmer and stir for about 2 minutes, until the sauce thickens. Add the chicken and stir to coat.

5. Garnish with the sesame seeds and scallions and serve over steamed rice.

HEAT CHECK: Use hot sesame oil if you'd prefer some spiciness.

Cashew Chicken

SERVES 2 TO 4 / PREP TIME: 10 MINUTES / COOK TIME: 10 MINUTES

30 MINUTES OR LESS

This dish was invented in 1963 by David Leong in Springfield, Missouri. Its popularity helped him open his own restaurant, which closed in 1997. In 2010, his son opened up his own restaurant.

---

2 tablespoons vegetable oil

3 garlic cloves, crushed and chopped

1 tablespoon crushed and chopped fresh ginger

1 medium carrot, roll cut into ½-inch pieces

1 pound boneless chicken thighs, cut into 1-inch cubes

1 medium onion, halved and cut into ½-inch slices

1 red bell pepper, diced into ½-inch pieces

1 cup dry-roasted cashews

1 cup chopped bok choy (about ½-inch pieces)

4 tablespoons soy sauce

2 tablespoons honey

1 tablespoon toasted sesame oil

1 teaspoon cornstarch

1 bunch (6 to 8) scallions, cut into ½-inch pieces

Steamed rice (see page 12), for serving

1. In a wok or large cast iron skillet, heat the vegetable oil over high heat, until it shimmers.

2. Add the garlic, ginger, and carrot and stir-fry for 1 minute. Add the chicken and onion and stir-fry for 1 minute. Add the bell pepper and cashews and stir-fry for 1 minute. Add the bok choy and stir-fry for 1 minute.

3. In a medium bowl, whisk together the soy sauce, honey, sesame oil, and cornstarch. Add the sauce to the wok, and stir for about 2 minutes, until a glaze forms.

4. Remove from the heat and stir in the scallions.

5. Serve over steamed rice.

TROUBLESHOOTING: Roll cut carrots by slicing a whole carrot into ½-inch pieces at a 45-degree angle and rolling it a quarter of a turn after each successive cut. These uniform slices have multiple cooking surfaces that stir-fry faster than disks.

Sichuan Chicken

SERVES 2 TO 4 / PREP TIME: 10 MINUTES / COOK TIME: 10 MINUTES

30 MINUTES OR LESS .

This popular, pungent, spicy dish gets its heat from dried chiles and the signature Sichuan peppercorns that produce an interesting, tingling numbness.

---

1 pound boneless chicken thighs, sliced into 1-inch cubes

¼ cup plus 1 tablespoon cornstarch, divided

1 teaspoon ground white pepper

½ cup vegetable oil

1 medium carrot, roll cut into ½-inch pieces

2 tablespoons crushed and chopped fresh ginger

4 garlic cloves, crushed and chopped

1 tablespoon ground Sichuan peppercorns

1 tablespoon red pepper flakes

1 medium red onion, diced into ½-inch pieces

1 red bell pepper, diced into ½-inch pieces

½ cup dry-roasted peanuts

1 bunch (6 to 8) scallions, cut into 1-inch pieces

3 tablespoons soy sauce

2 tablespoons rice wine

1 tablespoon brown sugar

1 teaspoon hot sesame oil

Steamed rice (see page 12), for serving

1. Seal the chicken, ¼ cup of cornstarch, and white pepper in a large zip-top bag and shake to coat evenly.

2. In a wok or large cast iron skillet, heat the vegetable oil over medium-high heat to 350°F, or until a wooden chopstick bubbles when placed in the oil.

3. Add the coated chicken and fry for about 3 minutes, until golden brown. Transfer the chicken to a plate.

4. Remove and discard all but 2 tablespoons of vegetable oil from the pan. Add the carrot and stir-fry for 2 minutes. Add the ginger, garlic, peppercorns, red pepper flakes, and onion and stir-fry for 1 minute. Add the bell pepper, peanuts, and scallions and stir-fry for 1 minute.

5. In a medium bowl, whisk together the soy sauce, rice wine, brown sugar, sesame oil, and the remaining 1 tablespoon of cornstarch. Add the sauce to the wok and stir for about 2 minutes, until a glaze forms. Add the chicken and stir to coat.

6. Serve over steamed rice.

HEAT CHECK: Increase or decrease the hot sesame oil and red pepper flakes to suit your spice preference.

Manchurian Chicken

SERVES 2 TO 4 / PREP TIME: 10 MINUTES / COOK TIME: 10 MINUTES

30 MINUTES OR LESS

This peppery Indo-Chinese fusion recipe was invented in Kolkata (Calcutta), India, by a Chinese chef named Nelson Wang. His invention launched a chain of restaurants in his native India and Nepal.

---

1 pound boneless chicken thighs, cut into 1-inch cubes

¼ cup cornstarch

1 teaspoon ground white pepper

½ cup oil

3 garlic cloves, crushed and chopped

1 tablespoon crushed and chopped fresh ginger

1 bunch (6 to 8) scallions, sliced

1 fresh chile, sliced

¼ cup ketchup

3 tablespoons soy sauce

Steamed rice (see page 12), for serving

1. Seal the chicken, cornstarch, and white pepper in a large zip-top bag and shake to coat evenly.

2. In a wok or large cast iron skillet, heat the oil over medium-high heat to 350°F, or until a wooden chopstick bubbles when placed in the oil.

3. Add the coated chicken and fry for about 3 minutes, until golden brown. Transfer the chicken to a plate.

4. Remove and discard all but 2 tablespoons of oil from the pan. Add the garlic and ginger and stir-fry for about 2 minutes, until lightly browned. Add the scallions and chile and stir-fry for 1 minute.

5. Stir in the ketchup and soy sauce. Add the chicken and stir to coat.

6. Serve over steamed rice.

HEAT CHECK: Increase or decrease the white pepper and chile to suit your spice preference.

Crispy Steamed Duck

SERVES 2 TO 4 / PREP TIME: 10 MINUTES / COOK TIME: 20 MINUTES

30 MINUTES OR LESS, GLUTEN-FREE

Duck is known for being a very fatty meat. Steaming the breast before frying it renders much of the fat while keeping the meat moist.

---

4 boneless, skin-on duck breasts

2 tablespoons cornstarch

1 tablespoon Chinese five-spice powder

5 scallions, sliced

Steamed rice (see page 12), noodles, or pancakes, for serving

Hoisin sauce, for dipping

1. Score the duck skin with shallow crosscuts about ¼ inch apart.

2. Place a wok or pot fitted with a steamer basket over high heat. Add enough water to come up 1 inch from the bottom of the basket. When the water boils, immediately place the duck, skin-side down, in the basket, cover, and steam for 10 minutes, or until the water is almost gone. Remove the duck and steamer basket, but leave the liquid.

3. Reduce the heat to medium for about 3 minutes more to evaporate the remaining water, leaving just the duck fat.

4. Transfer the duck to a large zip-top bag with the cornstarch and five-spice powder. Massage for 2 minutes.

5. Heat the duck fat over medium-high heat until it shimmers. Add the coated duck, skin-side up, and fry for 1 minute. Flip the duck over and fry for 2 minutes, or until the skin is crispy brown.

6. Thinly slice the duck, sprinkle it with scallions, and serve with steamed rice and hoisin sauce for dipping.

ALL HAIL THE PEKING DUCK

One of China's oldest and best-known dishes is the famous Peking duck. For thousands of years, this irresistible recipe has been prepared in restaurants by specially trained chefs. Ducks used for this recipe are young, well-fed, and raised specifically for the dish. The signature crispy skin is created by separating it from the body with compressed air prior to marinating the duck and roasting it in specially designed ovens. The roasted duck is then carved table side and served wrapped in thin pancakes along with slivered scallions and hoisin sauce. Historically prepared for royalty, Peking duck made national news in the United States as a result of President Richard Nixon's visit to China in 1972. It's been said that it was Henry Kissinger's love of Peking duck at a 12-course banquet that caused him to encourage Nixon to visit China.

BEEF AND BROCCOLI WITH OYSTER SAUCE, PAGE 66

CHAPTER FIVE

PORK, BEEF, AND LAMB

Legend has it that Chinese barbecue was discovered when a farmer's barn accidentally burned down. It's said that the smell and taste of the roasted meat caused the farmer to set his rebuilt barn on fire regularly after that. This chapter is a small introduction to some of China's tasty barbecue recipes. And you won't have to burn down any barns!

Red Cooked Pork (Hong Shao Rou)

SERVES 2 TO 4 / PREP TIME: 10 MINUTES / COOK TIME: 1 HOUR

This simple and tasty roast pork was Chairman Mao's favorite dish. The Chinese name literally means "red cooked pork."

---

1 pound pork belly or shoulder, cut into 1-inch pieces

2 tablespoons vegetable oil

4 garlic cloves, crushed and chopped

¼ cup sugar

¼ cup rice wine

3 tablespoons soy sauce

1 tablespoon Chinese five-spice powder

Steamed rice (see page 12), for serving

1. Place the pork in a wok or deep pot over medium-high heat. Add water to just cover the pork and bring it to a boil. Cook for 15 minutes, skimming any froth off the top.

2. Remove and strain the pork, reserving the broth.

3. In a wok or large cast iron skillet, heat the oil, garlic, and sugar over high heat for about 1 minute, until the sugar browns slightly. Add the strained pork and stir-fry for 2 to 3 minutes, until browned.

4. Add the reserved broth, rice wine, soy sauce, and five-spice powder and simmer over medium heat for 45 minutes, or until the pork is tender. Stir occasionally to be sure that the pork is not sticking to the bottom of the wok.

5. Serve over steamed rice.

Spicy Hoisin Pork

SERVES 2 TO 4 / PREP TIME: 10 MINUTES / COOK TIME: 20 MINUTES

30 MINUTES OR LESS

The thick hoisin sauce in this dish gives it a rich, slightly sweet and pungent flavor. Hot sesame oil adds a little spice.

---

1 pound Southern-style boneless pork ribs, cut into ¼-inch strips

3 tablespoons rice wine

1 tablespoon cornstarch

2 tablespoons avocado oil

1 medium carrot, roll cut into ½-inch pieces

3 garlic cloves, crushed and chopped

1 tablespoon crushed and chopped fresh ginger

1 medium red onion, diced into ½-inch pieces

1 red bell pepper, diced into ½-inch pieces

3 tablespoons soy sauce

3 tablespoons hoisin sauce

1 teaspoon hot sesame oil

1 bunch (6 to 8) scallions, cut into 1-inch pieces

Steamed rice (see page 12) or noodles, for serving

1. Seal the pork, rice wine, and cornstarch in a large zip-top bag. Massage for 2 minutes.

2. In a wok or large cast iron skillet, heat the oil over high heat until it shimmers. Add the carrot, garlic, and ginger and stir-fry for 1 minute. Add the onion and stir-fry for 1 minute. Add the marinated pork and stir-fry for 1 minute. Add the bell pepper and stir-fry for 1 minute.

3. Add the soy sauce, hoisin sauce, and sesame oil and stir for about 2 minutes, until a glaze forms.

4. Stir in the scallions and serve over steamed rice.

HEAT CHECK: Use more or less hot oil to regulate the spiciness.

Five-Spice Wok-Roasted Pork

SERVES 2 TO 4 / PREP TIME: 10 MINUTES / COOK TIME: 1 HOUR

This is a great way to prepare a pork roast. Using the wok allows the pork to marinate while it's roasting, keeping the meat very moist and tender. Although this recipe calls for loin roast, pork shoulder or beef brisket can be used with good results.

½ cup honey

¼ cup soy sauce

¼ cup ketchup

¼ cup rice wine

2 tablespoons Chinese five-spice powder

2 tablespoons crushed and chopped
   fresh ginger

1 tablespoon hot sesame oil

3 garlic cloves, crushed and chopped

1 (2- to 3-pound) pork loin roast

Rice and vegetables, for serving

1. Preheat the oven to 350°F.

2. In a medium bowl, whisk together the honey, soy sauce, ketchup, rice wine, five-spice powder, ginger, sesame oil, and garlic.

3. In wok or oven-safe bowl, rub the pork all over with the marinade.

4. Roast the pork in the preheated oven for 20 minutes. Turn the pork over and roast for 20 minutes more. Turn the pork over again and roast for a final 20 minutes, or until an instant-read thermometer inserted into the thickest part of the meat registers 145°F.

5. Let the pork rest for 3 minutes. Slice and serve with rice and vegetables.

TROUBLESHOOTING: Decreasing the heat by 100°F and cooking the pork for twice as long will result in more tenderness. Just remember to turn the meat over every 20 minutes.

Mapo Ground Pork and Tofu

SERVES 2 TO 4 / PREP TIME: 10 MINUTES / COOK TIME: 10 MINUTES

30 MINUTES OR LESS

This classic Sichuan dish combines the spicy heat of peppers and the numbing effect of ground Sichuan peppercorns. The word *mapo* means "pockmarked grandmother," apparently referring to the elderly woman who invented the dish!

---

2 tablespoons vegetable oil

½ pound ground pork

3 garlic cloves, crushed and chopped

1 tablespoon crushed and chopped fresh ginger

2 tablespoons Lee Kum Kee Spicy Bean Sauce

2 tablespoons ketchup

1 tablespoon cornstarch

1 bunch (6 to 8) scallions, cut into 1-inch pieces

1 teaspoon ground Sichuan peppercorns

1 teaspoon ground white pepper

1 teaspoon hot sesame oil

1 teaspoon red pepper flakes

1 cup chicken broth

1 pound silken tofu, cut into 1-inch cubes

Steamed rice (see page 12), for serving

1. In a wok or large cast iron skillet, heat the vegetable oil over high heat until it shimmers. Add the pork, garlic, and ginger and cook for about 2 minutes, until the pork is brown.

2. Add the bean sauce, ketchup, cornstarch, scallions, Sichuan peppercorns, white pepper, sesame oil, and red pepper flakes. Add the broth and stir for about 2 minutes, until the sauce thickens.

3. Reduce the heat to medium, then fold in the tofu. Cover and simmer for 5 minutes.

4. Serve over steamed rice.

HEAT CHECK: Use more or less hot sesame oil, spicy bean sauce, and red pepper flakes to regulate the heat.

Pork Spareribs with Black Bean Sauce

SERVES 2 TO 4 / PREP TIME: 10 MINUTES / COOK TIME: 50 MINUTES

Cutting the ribs in half to make bite-size pieces helps improve their flavor because more of the marrow cooks out of the bones and flavors the meat. Look for a butcher who will cut them for you. Ask them to separate the ribs when they saw the bones, or do it at home.

---

2 to 3 pounds baby back ribs, sawed in half and separated

2 tablespoons crushed and chopped fresh ginger

3 garlic cloves, crushed and chopped

¼ cup honey

¼ cup brown sugar

¼ cup Lee Kum Kee Black Bean Garlic Sauce

2 tablespoons soy sauce

1. Preheat the oven to 350°F and adjust a rack to the middle position. Line a baking dish with aluminum foil.

2. Combine the ribs, ginger, garlic, honey, brown sugar, bean sauce, and soy sauce in the prepared baking dish so that the ribs are in a single layer, just touching one another and the sides of the pan.

3. Roast the ribs on the middle rack of the preheated oven for 30 minutes. Turn the ribs over and roast for 20 minutes more, or until an instant-read thermometer inserted into the thickest part of the meat registers 145°F.

4. Serve alone or over rice.

TROUBLESHOOTING: Make the meat more tender by lowering the temperature by 100°F and cooking the ribs between 2 and 3 hours longer. Just remember to turn the meat over every 20 minutes.

Steamed Pork and Cabbage

(Yook Beng)

SERVES 2 TO 4 / PREP TIME: 10 MINUTES / COOK TIME: 15 MINUTES

30 MINUTES OR LESS

This steamed pork meatloaf is a blast from my childhood. The cabbage takes the place of bread in a traditional American meatloaf. My mother used American cabbage because it was the only kind available in the local suburban grocery store.

½ pound ground pork

2 cups chopped cabbage

4 large eggs

¼ cup soy sauce

2 tablespoons crushed and chopped fresh ginger

3 garlic cloves, crushed and chopped

1 bunch (6 to 8) scallions, chopped, divided

Steamed rice (see page 12), for serving

1. Use a Chinese cleaver or chef's knife to coarsely chop together the pork, cabbage, eggs, soy sauce, ginger, garlic, and half of the scallions until the mixture is flattened and uniform on your cutting board.

2. Loosely place the pork mixture into 2 pie pans. Do not pack the mixture down.

3. Place a wok or pot fitted with a steamer basket over high heat. Add enough water to come up 1 inch from the bottom of the basket. When the water boils, immediately place the pie pans in the basket, cover, and steam for 15 minutes.

4. Garnish with the remaining half of the scallions and serve over steamed rice.

SUBSTITUTION TIP: You could make a 50/50 mix of shrimp and pork or scallops and pork for a seafood variation of this recipe.

Beef and Broccoli with Oyster Sauce

SERVES 2 TO 4 / PREP TIME: 10 MINUTES / COOK TIME: 8 MINUTES

30 MINUTES OR LESS

The thick oyster sauce in this easy stir-fry adds a rich, sweet flavor to the meat and vegetables.

---

2 tablespoons vegetable oil

1 medium onion, diced into ½-inch pieces

1 tablespoon crushed and chopped fresh ginger

3 garlic cloves, crushed and chopped

1 pound sirloin strip steak, thinly sliced

4 ounces white or portobello mushrooms, sliced

2 cups sliced broccoli florets

1 red bell pepper, diced into ½-inch pieces

3 tablespoons soy sauce

1 tablespoon rice wine

¼ cup oyster sauce

1 bunch (6 to 8) scallions, cut into ½-inch pieces

Steamed rice (see page 12) or noodles, for serving

1. In a wok or large cast iron skillet, heat the oil over high heat until it shimmers. Add the onion, ginger, and garlic and stir-fry for about 1 minute, until lightly browned.

2. Add the steak and stir-fry for 1 minute. Add the mushrooms and stir-fry for 1 minute. Add the broccoli and stir-fry for 1 minute. Add the bell pepper and stir-fry for 1 minute.

3. Add the soy sauce, rice wine, and oyster sauce and stir-fry for 1 minute.

4. Stir in the scallions and serve over steamed rice.

SUBSTITUTION TIP: If you're out of oyster sauce, substitute it with ¼ cup of hoisin sauce.

Mongolian Beef

30 MINUTES OR LESS

This popular sweet and salty stir-fry was invented in Taiwan. The sauce is similar to Chinese barbecue sauce, but it's not as thick and sweet.

---

1 pound sirloin strip steak, thinly sliced

4 tablespoons cornstarch, divided

2 tablespoons rice wine

2 tablespoons vegetable oil

2 tablespoons crushed and chopped fresh ginger

3 garlic cloves, crushed and chopped

¼ cup honey

¼ cup ketchup

2 tablespoons soy sauce

1 teaspoon hot sesame oil

1 bunch (6 to 8) scallions, cut into ½-inch pieces

1 teaspoon sesame seeds

Steamed rice (see page 12), for serving

1. In a medium bowl, combine the steak, 3 tablespoons of cornstarch, and rice wine. Massage to coat evenly.

2. In a wok or large cast iron skillet, heat the vegetable oil over high heat until it shimmers. Add the ginger and garlic and stir-fry for about 1 minute, until lightly browned.

3. Add the steak and stir-fry for 2 minutes.

4. In a medium bowl, whisk together the honey, ketchup, soy sauce, sesame oil, and the remaining 1 tablespoon of cornstarch. Add the sauce to the wok and cook for about 2 minutes, until it thickens.

5. Garnish with the scallions and sesame seeds and serve over steamed rice.

Sichuan Beef and Vegetables

SERVES 2 TO 4 / PREP TIME: 10 MINUTES / COOK TIME: 10 MINUTES

30 MINUTES OR LESS

This hot-spicy dish combines the heat of red pepper flakes and hot sesame oil with the numbing effect of ground Sichuan peppercorns. If you want to be woken up and clear your head, this recipe is for you!

---

1 pound sirloin strip steak, thinly sliced

3 tablespoons soy sauce

2 tablespoons cornstarch, divided

2 tablespoons vegetable oil

2 tablespoons crushed and chopped fresh ginger

3 garlic cloves, crushed and chopped

1 medium onion, diced into ½-inch pieces

1 red bell pepper, diced into ½-inch pieces

1 teaspoon red pepper flakes

3 tablespoons Lee Kum Kee Black Bean Garlic Sauce

2 tablespoons rice wine

1 tablespoon hot sesame oil

1 teaspoon ground Sichuan peppercorns

1 bunch (6 to 8) scallions, cut into 1-inch pieces

1 teaspoon sesame seeds

Steamed rice (see page 12), for serving

1. Seal the steak, soy sauce, and 1 tablespoon of cornstarch in a large zip-top bag. Massage for 2 minutes.

2. In a wok or large cast iron skillet, heat the vegetable oil over high heat until it shimmers. Add the ginger and garlic and stir-fry for about 1 minute, until lightly browned.

3. Add the onion and stir-fry for 1 minute. Add the marinated steak and stir-fry for 1 minute. Add the bell pepper and red pepper flakes and stir-fry for 1 minute.

4. In a medium bowl, whisk together the bean sauce, rice wine, sesame oil, peppercorns, and the remaining 1 tablespoon of cornstarch. Add the sauce to the wok and cook for about 2 minutes, until it thickens.

5. Garnish with the scallions and sesame seeds and serve over steamed rice.

HEAT CHECK: Use more or less hot sesame oil and red pepper flakes to regulate the heat.

Sesame Ginger Beef

SERVES 2 TO 4 / PREP TIME: 10 MINUTES / COOK TIME: 10 MINUTES

30 MINUTES OR LESS

In this savory and slightly sweet stir-fry, mushrooms add an umami flavor while fresh green beans provide some color and crunch.

---

1 pound sirloin strip steak, thinly sliced

4 tablespoons cornstarch, divided

2 tablespoons rice wine

2 tablespoons vegetable oil

3 tablespoons crushed and chopped fresh ginger

2 garlic cloves, crushed and chopped

8 ounces green beans

4 ounces white mushrooms, sliced

1 red bell pepper, diced into ½-inch pieces

¼ cup soy sauce

2 tablespoons sugar

1 tablespoon rice vinegar

1 tablespoon toasted or hot sesame oil

1 bunch (6 to 8) scallions, cut into ½-inch pieces

1 teaspoon sesame seeds

Steamed rice (see page 12), for serving

1. Seal the steak, 3 tablespoons of cornstarch, and rice wine in a large zip-top bag. Massage for 2 minutes.

2. In a wok or large cast iron skillet, heat the vegetable oil over high heat until it shimmers. Add the ginger and garlic and stir-fry for about 1 minute, until lightly browned.

3. Add the green beans and stir-fry for 1 minute. Add the marinated steak and stir-fry for 1 minute. Add the mushrooms and stir-fry for 1 minute. Add the bell pepper and stir-fry for 1 minute.

4. In a medium bowl, whisk together the soy sauce, sugar, vinegar, sesame oil, and the remaining 1 tablespoon of cornstarch. Add the sauce to the wok and cook for about 2 minutes, until a glaze forms.

5. Garnish with the scallions and sesame seeds and serve over steamed rice.

SUBSTITUTION TIP: Try substituting ground pork or sliced chicken in this recipe.

Kung Pao Beef

SERVES 2 TO 4 / PREP TIME: 10 MINUTES / COOK TIME: 10 MINUTES

30 MINUTES OR LESS

In Chinese, the term *kung pao* means "palace guardian." This dish was named after Ding Baozhen, who was a governor of the Sichuan Province. True to its roots, kung pao is a spicy dish with sweet and sour flavors.

---

1 pound sirloin strip steak, thinly sliced

4 tablespoons cornstarch, divided

2 tablespoons sugar

1 tablespoon soy sauce

1 teaspoon ground Sichuan peppercorns

2 tablespoons vegetable oil

3 tablespoons crushed and chopped fresh ginger

2 garlic cloves, crushed and chopped

1 red bell pepper, diced into ½-inch pieces

1 tablespoon Guilin chili paste

2 tablespoons rice vinegar

1 tablespoon rice wine

1 teaspoon hot sesame oil

1 bunch (6 to 8) scallions, cut into ½-inch pieces

Steamed rice (see page 12), for serving

1. Seal the steak, 3 tablespoons of cornstarch, sugar, soy sauce, and peppercorns in a large zip-top bag. Massage for 2 minutes.

2. In a wok or large cast iron skillet, heat the vegetable oil over high heat until it shimmers. Add the ginger and garlic and stir-fry for about 1 minute, until lightly browned.

3. Add the marinated steak and stir-fry for 1 minute. Add the bell pepper, chili paste, vinegar, rice wine, and sesame oil and stir-fry for 1 minute. Add the scallions and stir-fry for 1 minute.

4. Add the remaining 1 tablespoon of cornstarch and mix for about 2 minutes, until a galaze forms.

5. Serve over steamed rice.

HEAT CHECK: Use more or less chili paste and hot sesame oil to regulate the heat.

Beef and Peppers with Black Bean Sauce

SERVES 2 TO 4 / PREP TIME: 10 MINUTES / COOK TIME: 10 MINUTES

30 MINUTES OR LESS

This is a quick and simple stir-fry with beef and vegetables. The fermented black bean garlic sauce provides a little spiciness, glaze, and umami flavor.

---

1 pound sirloin strip steak, thinly sliced

1 tablespoon sugar

1 tablespoon soy sauce

1 tablespoon cornstarch

3 tablespoons rice wine, divided

2 tablespoons vegetable oil

3 tablespoons crushed and chopped fresh ginger

2 garlic cloves, crushed and chopped

1 medium onion, cut into ½-inch dice

1 red bell pepper, cut into ½-inch dice

1 green bell pepper, cut into ½-inch dice

1 bunch (6 to 8) scallions, cut into 1-inch pieces

¼ cup Lee Kum Kee Black Bean Garlic Sauce

Steamed rice (see page 12) or noodles, for serving

1. Seal the steak, sugar, soy sauce, cornstarch, and 1 tablespoon of rice wine in a large zip-top bag. Massage for 2 minutes.

2. In a wok or large cast iron skillet, heat the oil over high heat until it shimmers. Add the ginger and garlic and stir-fry for about 1 minute, until lightly browned.

3. Add the marinated steak and stir-fry for 1 minute. Add the onion and stir-fry for 1 minute. Add the red and green bell peppers and stir-fry for 1 minute. Add the scallions and stir-fry for 1 minute.

4. Add the bean sauce and the remaining 2 tablespoons of rice wine and stir-fry for 1 minute.

5. Serve over steamed rice.

Beef and Snow Peas
with Oyster Sauce

SERVES 2 TO 4 / PREP TIME: 10 MINUTES / COOK TIME: 10 MINUTES

30 MINUTES OR LESS

This is a classic, quick, and easy stir-fry where the oyster sauce does all the heavy lifting in terms of flavor and glaze.

---

1 pound sirloin strip steak, thinly sliced

1 tablespoon sugar

1 tablespoon rice wine

1 tablespoon cornstarch

2 tablespoons vegetable oil

3 tablespoons crushed and chopped fresh ginger

2 garlic cloves, crushed and chopped

1 medium onion, cut into ¼-inch strips

24 snow peas or sugar snap peas

1 bunch (6 to 8) scallions, cut into 1-inch pieces

¼ cup oyster sauce

Steamed rice (see page 12) or noodles, for serving

1. Seal the steak, sugar, rice wine, and cornstarch in a large zip-top bag. Massage for 2 minutes.

2. In a wok or large cast iron skillet, heat the oil over high heat until it shimmers. Add the ginger and garlic and stir-fry for about 1 minute, until lightly browned.

3. Add the marinated steak and stir-fry for 1 minute. Add the onion and stir-fry for 1 minute. Add the snow peas and stir-fry for 1 minute. Add the scallions and stir-fry for 1 minute. Add the oyster sauce and stir-fry for 1 minute.

4. Serve over steamed rice.

SUBSTITUTION TIP: If someone is allergic to oyster sauce, replace it with my Vegetarian Oyster Sauce (see page 125).

Lamb in Black Pepper Sauce

SERVES 2 TO 4 / PREP TIME: 10 MINUTES / COOK TIME: 6 MINUTES

30 MINUTES OR LESS

This is a spicy and sweet dish. The key here is to avoid overcooking the lamb, as it will easily dry out and get tough.

1 pound boneless lamb sirloin, cut across the grain into ¼-inch strips

1 tablespoon soy sauce

1 tablespoon rice wine

1 tablespoon cornstarch

1 teaspoon Chinese five-spice powder

2 tablespoons vegetable oil

3 garlic cloves, crushed and chopped

1 tablespoon crushed and chopped fresh ginger

1 teaspoon freshly ground black pepper

1 teaspoon ground Sichuan peppercorns

1 bunch (6 to 8) scallions, cut into ½-inch pieces

¼ cup oyster sauce

1 teaspoon hot sesame oil

Steamed rice (see page 12) or noodles, for serving

1. Seal the lamb, soy sauce, rice wine, cornstarch, and five-spice powder in a large zip-top bag. Massage for 2 minutes.

2. In a wok or large cast iron skillet, heat the vegetable oil over high heat until it shimmers. Add the garlic and ginger and stir-fry for about 1 minute, until lightly browned.

3. Add the marinated lamb and stir-fry for 30 seconds. Add the black pepper and Sichuan peppercorns and stir-fry for 30 seconds. Add the scallions and stir-fry for 30 seconds.

4. Add the oyster sauce and sesame oil and stir-fry for 30 seconds.

5. Serve over steamed rice.

SUBSTITUTION TIP: Pork or beef could be substituted for the lamb.

SWEET AND SOUR SHRIMP, PAGE 77

CHAPTER SIX

SEAFOOD

Representing wealth and abundance, the fish is one of the oldest animal symbols in China. Spectral analysis of 40,000-year-old skeletal remains in Asia indicate that seafood was consumed regularly in ancient China. The Chinese invented aquaculture in the first millennium BCE. The recipes in this chapter are a small sample of that legacy.

Shrimp with Lobster Sauce

SERVES 2 TO 4 / PREP TIME: 10 MINUTES / COOK TIME: 10 MINUTES

30 MINUTES OR LESS

There is no lobster in this dish! This Cantonese recipe was originally made to accompany lobster in Chinese American restaurants. But because of fresh lobster's high price and low accessibility, shrimp became a popular substitute.

---

2 tablespoons vegetable oil

3 garlic cloves, crushed and chopped

1 tablespoon crushed and chopped fresh ginger

½ pound ground pork

½ pound medium shrimp, peeled and deveined

1 tablespoon rice wine

1 cup chicken stock

2 tablespoons cornstarch

2 tablespoons soy sauce

1 teaspoon hot sesame oil

1 teaspoon sugar

½ cup frozen peas, thawed

2 large eggs, beaten

4 scallions, cut into ½-inch pieces

Steamed rice (see page 12), for serving

1. In a wok or large cast iron skillet, heat the vegetable oil over high heat until it shimmers. Add the garlic and ginger and stir-fry for about 1 minute, until lightly browned.

2. Add the pork and stir-fry for 2 minutes. Add the shrimp and rice wine and stir-fry for 1 minute.

3. In a medium bowl, whisk together the chicken stock, cornstarch, soy sauce, sesame oil, and sugar. Add the sauce to the wok and cook for about 2 minutes, until it thickens and a light glaze forms.

4. Add the peas and stir-fry for 1 minute. Drizzle in the eggs and stir-fry for 1 minute.

5. Gently fold in the scallions and serve over steamed rice.

SUBSTITUTION TIP: This recipe is also very good with sea scallops.

Sweet and Sour Shrimp

SERVES 2 TO 4 / PREP TIME: 10 MINUTES / COOK TIME: 10 MINUTES

30 MINUTES OR LESS, GLUTEN-FREE, SOY-FREE

This stir-fry combines fresh, crisp vegetables with healthy seafood. The light and tangy sweetness of the pineapple will wake up your taste buds for sure!

---

2 tablespoons vegetable oil

3 garlic cloves, crushed and chopped

1 tablespoon crushed and chopped fresh ginger

1 medium onion, diced into ½-inch pieces

1 pound medium shrimp, shelled and deveined

1 red bell pepper, diced into ½-inch pieces

1 (20-ounce) can chunk pineapple

2 tablespoons rice vinegar

2 tablespoons ketchup

2 tablespoons cornstarch

1 bunch (6 to 8) scallions, cut into ½-inch pieces

Steamed rice (see page 12) or noodles, for serving

1. In a wok or large cast iron skillet, heat the vegetable oil over high heat until it shimmers. Add the garlic and ginger and stir-fry for about 1 minute, until lightly browned.

2. Add the onion and stir-fry for 1 minute. Add the shrimp and bell pepper and stir-fry for 1 minute.

3. In a medium bowl, whisk together the pineapple chunks with their juices, vinegar, ketchup, and cornstarch. Add the sauce to the wok and cook for about 2 minutes, until it thickens and a glaze forms.

4. Fold in the scallions and serve over steamed rice.

SUBSTITUTION TIP: You can substitute balsamic or cider vinegar for the rice vinegar in this recipe.

Sesame Shrimp

SERVES 2 TO 4 / PREP TIME: 10 MINUTES / COOK TIME: 6 MINUTES

30 MINUTES OR LESS

This quick stir-fry combines the natural sweetness of shrimp with the nutty flavor of sesame oil. The light glaze keeps the shrimp moist and is not overpowering.

---

2 tablespoons vegetable oil

2 tablespoons crushed and chopped fresh ginger

3 garlic cloves, crushed and chopped

1 medium onion, diced into ½-inch pieces

1 pound medium shrimp, peeled, deveined, and cut completely down the middle

1 red bell pepper, diced into ½-inch pieces

3 tablespoons soy sauce

3 tablespoons rice wine

3 tablespoons sugar

1 tablespoon toasted or hot sesame oil

1 tablespoon cornstarch

1 bunch (6 to 8) scallions, cut into ½-inch pieces

1 teaspoon sesame seeds

Steamed rice (see page 12) or noodles, for serving

1. In a wok or large cast iron skillet, heat the vegetable oil over high heat until it shimmers. Add the ginger and garlic and stir-fry for about 1 minute, until lightly browned.

2. Add the onion and stir-fry for 1 minute. Add the shrimp and stir-fry for 1 minute. Add the bell pepper and stir-fry for 1 minute.

3. In a medium bowl, whisk together the soy sauce, rice wine, sugar, sesame oil, and cornstarch. Add the sauce to the wok and cook, stirring, for about 2 minutes, until a glaze forms.

4. Add the scallions and stir for 30 seconds.

5. Garnish with the sesame seeds and serve over steamed rice.

Honey Walnut Shrimp

SERVES 2 TO 4 / PREP TIME: 10 MINUTES / COOK TIME: 10 MINUTES

30 MINUTES OR LESS

This savory seafood recipe originated in Hong Kong. It is based on the Cantonese flavor base of ginger, garlic, and scallions.

---

1 cup water

1 cup sugar

1 cup walnuts

1 large egg, beaten

¼ cup cornstarch

1 teaspoon kosher salt

½ teaspoon ground white pepper

1 pound medium shrimp, peeled and deveined

¼ cup vegetable oil

2 tablespoons crushed and chopped fresh ginger

3 garlic cloves, crushed and chopped

1 medium onion, diced into ½-inch pieces

1 red bell pepper, diced into ½-inch pieces

1 bunch (6 to 8) scallions, cut into ½-inch pieces

¼ cup honey

¼ cup mayonnaise

2 tablespoons rice wine

2 tablespoons soy sauce

Steamed rice (see page 12), for serving

1. In a small pan, heat the water and sugar over medium-high heat until the water boils and the sugar dissolves.

2. Add the walnuts and boil for 1 minute. Transfer the walnuts to paper towels to drain.

3. Place the egg in a small bowl. In another small bowl, combine the cornstarch, salt, and white pepper.

4. Dip the shrimp in the egg, one at a time, to coat, then dredge in the cornstarch mixture, coating evenly.

5. In a wok or large cast iron skillet, heat the oil over high heat until it shimmers. Add the coated shrimp and stir-fry for about 3 minutes, until golden brown. Transfer the fried shrimp to a plate.

6. Remove and discard all but 2 tablespoons of oil from the pan. Add the ginger and garlic and stir-fry for about 1 minute, until lightly browned.

continued

Honey Walnut Shrimp *continued*

7. Add the onion and stir-fry for 1 minute. Add the bell pepper and stir-fry for 1 minute. Add the scallions and stir-fry for 1 minute.

8. In a medium bowl, whisk together the honey, mayonnaise, rice wine, and soy sauce. Add the sauce to the wok and cook, stirring, for about 2 minutes, until a glaze forms. Add the walnuts and shrimp, tossing to coat.

9. Serve over steamed rice.

SUBSTITUTION TIP: Substituting maple syrup for the honey makes a great variation on this recipe.

Cantonese Steamed Fish Fillet

SERVES 2 TO 4 / PREP TIME: 5 MINUTES / COOK TIME: 10 MINUTES

30 MINUTES OR LESS

This is a fast and easy way to cook up a fish that looks great and maintains all of its natural juices and flavor.

---

1 pound fish fillet, such as tilapia, haddock, salmon, or cod

2 tablespoons rice wine

2 tablespoons crushed and chopped fresh ginger

3 garlic cloves, crushed and chopped

2 tablespoons soy sauce

1 tablespoon toasted or hot sesame oil

1 bunch (6 to 8) scallions, cut into ¼-inch pieces

Steamed rice (see page 12), for serving

1. Place the fish on a plate or platter and score 1-inch crosscuts into its skin with a knife.

2. Transfer the scored fish to a wok or pot fitted with a steamer basket. Add enough water to come up 1 inch from the bottom of the basket.

3. In a medium bowl, whisk together the rice wine, ginger, garlic, soy sauce, sesame oil, and scallions. Drizzle the sauce over the fish, pressing the scallions, ginger, and garlic gently into the scored cuts.

4. Set the wok over high heat and bring the water to a brisk boil, then cover and steam for 5 to 7 minutes, until the fish is flaky and opaque.

5. Serve over steamed rice.

TROUBLESHOOTING: Do not lift the lid while your meal steams. It decreases the temperature inside the wok and affects cooking.

Whole Fried Fish

SERVES 2 TO 4 / PREP TIME: 10 MINUTES / COOK TIME: 10 MINUTES

30 MINUTES OR LESS

This is the highlight of all Chinese banquets and special occasions. The fish represents good luck and prosperity. The head always points to the head of the family or the guest of honor. If you want good luck, eat one of the eyes.

---

1 (1- to 2-pound) fish, such as tilapia, whole, cleaned and scaled

1 cup vegetable oil

3 tablespoons crushed and chopped fresh ginger

5 garlic cloves, crushed and chopped

2 tablespoons soy sauce

2 tablespoons rice wine

1 tablespoon Chinese five-spice powder

1 teaspoon hot sesame oil

1 bunch (6 to 8) scallions, cut into ½-inch pieces

Steamed rice (see page 12), for serving

1. Pat the fish dry to reduce splatter when frying. Cut shallow, diagonal slits just below the skin across both sides of the fish. The cuts should be about 1 inch apart.

2. In a wok or shallow pan large enough to hold the fish, heat the vegetable oil to 350°F, or until a wooden chopstick bubbles when placed in the vegetable oil.

3. Add the ginger and garlic and fry for about 1 minute, until lightly browned.

4. Carefully slide the fish into the vegetable oil and fry for 2 minutes on one side. Turn the fish over and fry for 2 minutes on the other side, or until the fish is flaky and opaque.

5. Remove and discard all but 2 tablespoons of vegetable oil from the pan, keeping the fish in the pan. Reduce the heat to medium.

6. In a medium bowl, whisk together the soy sauce, rice wine, five-spice powder, and sesame oil. Pour half the sauce around the fish and cook for 1 minute, until the flavors meld.

7. Turn the fish over and pour the remaining half of the sauce around the fish. Cook for 1 minute more.

8. Transfer the fish to a serving platter.

9. Add the scallions to the wok with the sauce and stir-fry for 1 minute. Pour the sauce and scallions over the fish.

10. Serve with steamed rice.

SUBSTITUTION TIP: Many types of fish are great for this recipe. Try red snapper, porgy, sea bass, or rockfish.

TAKE A SHORTCUT: You don't have to clean and scale the fish yourself. Ask the fish monger to do it at the fish market before you take it home.

Cast Iron Salmon Fillet with Hoisin Sauce

SERVES 2 TO 4 / PREP TIME: 10 MINUTES / COOK TIME: 20 MINUTES

30 MINUTES OR LESS, GLUTEN-FREE

This is my favorite way to cook large fish fillets and whole fish. Heating up the cast iron griddle under the broiler cooks the fish on both sides, so you won't need to turn it.

---

2 tablespoons vegetable oil

½ cup hoisin sauce

¼ cup honey

2 tablespoons rice wine

1 teaspoon hot sesame oil

3 tablespoons crushed and chopped fresh ginger

4 garlic cloves, crushed and chopped

1 bunch (6 to 8) scallions, cut into ¼-inch pieces

1 (1- to 2-pound) salmon fillet

Steamed rice (see page 12), for serving

1. Grease a cast iron or oven-safe griddle or pan with the vegetable oil. Place the griddle 2 to 3 inches under the broiler element, set the broiler to high, and let the griddle heat for 5 to 10 minutes, or until it just begins to smoke.

2. In a medium bowl, whisk together the hoisin sauce, honey, rice wine, and sesame oil. Then, whisk in the ginger, garlic, and scallions.

3. Make shallow crosscuts in the fish about 1 inch apart. Gently press the sauce into the cuts.

4. Place the fish on the griddle and broil for 5 to 7 minutes for medium rare.

5. Serve with steamed rice.

SUBSTITUTION TIP: Substituting maple syrup for the honey makes a great variation on this recipe.

Sichuan Scallops

SERVES 2 TO 4 / PREP TIME: 10 MINUTES / COOK TIME: 6 MINUTES

30 MINUTES OR LESS

This quick and tasty seafood stir-fry has a bit of a bite. It's best to use fresh sea scallops.

---

2 tablespoons vegetable oil

3 garlic cloves, crushed and chopped

1 tablespoon crushed and chopped fresh ginger

1 medium onion, diced into ½-inch pieces

1 red bell pepper, diced into ½-inch pieces

¾ pound large sea scallops, halved coin-wise

2 tablespoons soy sauce

1 tablespoon sugar

1 tablespoon ground Sichuan peppercorns

1 tablespoon rice wine

1 tablespoon cornstarch

1 teaspoon red pepper flakes

1 teaspoon hot sesame oil

Steamed rice (see page 12), for serving

1. In a wok or large cast iron skillet, heat the vegetable oil over high heat until it shimmers. Add the garlic and ginger and stir-fry for about 1 minute, until lightly browned.

2. Add the onion and stir-fry for 1 minute. Add the bell pepper and stir-fry for 1 minute. Add the scallops and stir-fry for 1 minute.

3. In a medium bowl, whisk together the soy sauce, sugar, peppercorns, rice wine, cornstarch, red pepper flakes, and sesame oil. Add the sauce to the wok and cook, stirring, for about 2 minutes, until a glaze forms.

4. Serve over steamed rice.

TROUBLESHOOTING: If you can't get fresh sea scallops, defrost frozen scallops overnight in the refrigerator. You can also defrost them in cool running water securely sealed in a zip-top bag.

Garlic Scallops

SERVES 2 TO 4 / PREP TIME: 10 MINUTES / COOK TIME: 10 MINUTES

30 MINUTES OR LESS

Fresh sea scallops, bright red sweet peppers, and green scallions set the stage for an amazing meal that's ready in about 10 minutes—as long as your rice or noodles are ready!

---

2 tablespoons vegetable oil

2 tablespoons crushed and chopped fresh ginger

4 garlic cloves, crushed and chopped

1 medium onion, diced into ½-inch pieces

1 red bell pepper, diced into ½-inch pieces

¾ pound large sea scallops, halved coin-wise

2 tablespoons rice wine

2 tablespoons soy sauce

1 tablespoon Lee Kum Kee Black Bean Garlic Sauce

1 bunch (6 to 8) scallions, cut into ½-inch pieces

Steamed rice (see page 12), for serving

1. In a wok or large cast iron skillet, heat the vegetable oil over high heat until it shimmers. Add the ginger and garlic and stir-fry for about 1 minute, until lightly browned.

2. Add the onion and stir-fry for 1 minute. Add the bell pepper and stir-fry for 1 minute. Add the scallops and stir-fry for 1 minute.

3. In a medium bowl, whisk together the rice wine, soy sauce, and bean sauce. Add the sauce to the wok and cook, stirring, for about 2 minutes, until a glaze forms.

4. Add the scallions and stir-fry for 1 minute.

5. Serve over steamed rice.

TROUBLESHOOTING: Halving the large sea scallops into two coins allows them to cook evenly and quickly. They are done when they are opaque and slightly cracked around the edges.

Steamed Mussels and Clams with Oyster Sauce

SERVES 2 TO 4 / PREP TIME: 10 MINUTES / COOK TIME: 20 MINUTES

30 MINUTES OR LESS

This is another classic Cantonese seafood dish. Do not use soft-shelled clams, as their necks have a tough sheath that needs to be removed before eating them.

---

1 pound fresh mussels

2 pounds hard-shelled clams, such as littlenecks, mahogany, or cherrystones

½ cup rice wine

¼ cup soy sauce

3 tablespoons crushed and chopped fresh ginger

5 garlic cloves, crushed and chopped

½ cup oyster sauce

Steamed rice (see page 12), for serving

Steamed, roasted, or stir-fried vegetables, for serving

1. Thoroughly clean and debeard the shells of the mussels and clams with cold water and a brush.

2. In a wok or large cast iron skillet over high heat, combine the rice wine, soy sauce, ginger, and garlic. Add the mussels and clams. Cover, bring to a boil, and steam for 5 to 7 minutes, or until all the shells are open.

3. Transfer the shells to a shallow serving bowl, reserving the liquid in the wok.

4. Add the oyster sauce to the wok and simmer, stirring, for 2 minutes, until well incorporated.

5. Drizzle the sauce over the mussels and clams.

6. Serve over steamed rice with vegetables.

TROUBLESHOOTING: If a shell does not close when tapped or does not open after being cooked, discard it.

BOK CHOY WITH
CRISPY TOFU,
PAGE 95

CHAPTER SEVEN

VEGETABLES, TOFU, AND EGGS

Chinese farmers started cultivating rice over 9,000 years ago; tofu was invented in China over 2,000 years ago; and eggs have been collected from chickens, ducks, and geese for over 3,000 years. With these ingredients, there are many good reasons to eat your Chinese vegetables!

Roasted Sichuan Eggplant and Green Beans

SERVES 2 TO 4 / PREP TIME: 5 MINUTES / COOK TIME: 10 MINUTES

30 MINUTES OR LESS, VEGETARIAN

As with all stir-frying, whenever you have ingredients that cook at different rates, start with the ingredients that take longer to cook, followed by the more tender ingredients. Timing and order matters!

---

1 Chinese eggplant, roll cut into ½-inch pieces

1 tablespoon kosher salt

1 teaspoon ground white pepper

2 tablespoons vegetable oil

½ pound green beans, trimmed and cut into 2-inch pieces

2 tablespoons soy sauce

2 tablespoons rice wine

1 tablespoon Chinese five-spice powder

1 teaspoon red pepper flakes

1 teaspoon hot sesame oil

1. Place a large cast iron skillet or oven-safe pan 2 to 3 inches under the broiler element, turn on the broiler, and let the skillet heat for 5 minutes.

2. Spread the eggplant in a single layer in the skillet and broil for 5 minutes. Add the salt, white pepper, and vegetable oil, tossing to coat evenly. Add the green beans, soy sauce, rice wine, five-spice powder, red pepper flakes, and sesame oil, tossing to coat evenly.

3. Stir everything together and spread the mixture out evenly in the skillet. Broil for 5 minutes, or until the green beans blister and are slightly charred.

4. Serve immediately.

TROUBLESHOOTING: Do not overload the pan. Spread the vegetables in a single layer to ensure that they roast rather than steam.

Steamed Broccoli with Oyster Sauce

SERVES 2 TO 4 / PREP TIME: 10 MINUTES / COOK TIME: 20 MINUTES

30 MINUTES OR LESS, VEGETARIAN

Steaming broccoli (or any other veggie) is a quick and easy way to prepare it while preserving as much of its taste and nutrition as possible.

Chinese or regular broccoli, trimmed and cut into 2-inch florets

¼ cup Vegetarian Oyster Sauce (see page 125)

1. Place a wok or pot fitted with a steamer basket over high heat. Add enough water to come up 1 inch from the bottom of the basket. When the water boils, immediately place the broccoli in the basket, cover, and steam for 5 minutes.

2. Transfer the broccoli to a serving bowl and toss it with the oyster sauce.

Eggplant with Garlic Sauce

SERVES 2 TO 4 / PREP TIME: 10 MINUTES / COOK TIME: 10 MINUTES

30 MINUTES OR LESS, VEGETARIAN

Chinese eggplants are thinner and more tender than Western eggplants. If you use Western eggplants, select small ripe ones and peel them before cooking.

---

1 teaspoon kosher salt

2 tablespoons water

2 to 3 Chinese eggplants, roll cut into 1-inch pieces

4 tablespoons cornstarch, divided

2 tablespoons vegetable oil

2 tablespoons crushed and chopped fresh ginger

4 garlic cloves, crushed and chopped

¼ cup rice wine

3 tablespoons Lee Kum Kee Black Bean Garlic Sauce

2 tablespoons soy sauce

1 tablespoon sugar

1 bunch (6 to 8) scallions, cut into ¼-inch slices

Steamed rice (see page 12), for serving

1. In a small bowl, dissolve the salt in the water. Then, seal the salt water, eggplant, and 3 tablespoons of cornstarch in a large zip-top bag. Shake until evenly coated.

2. In a wok or large cast iron skillet, heat the oil over high heat until it shimmers. Add the ginger and garlic and stir-fry for about 1 minute, until lightly browned.

3. Add the coated eggplant and stir-fry for 5 minutes, until golden brown.

4. In a medium bowl, whisk together the rice wine, bean sauce, soy sauce, sugar, and the remaining 1 tablespoon of cornstarch. Add the sauce to the wok and cook, stirring, for about 2 minutes, until it thickens and a glaze forms.

5. Garnish with the scallions and serve over steamed rice.

TROUBLESHOOTING: Roll cut eggplant by slicing a whole eggplant into 1-inch pieces at a 45-degree angle and rolling it a quarter of a turn after each successive cut. The uniform pieces will have multiple cooking surfaces that stir-fry faster than disks.

Sichuan Dry-Roasted Green Beans

SERVES 2 TO 4 / PREP TIME: 5 MINUTES / COOK TIME: 5 MINUTES

30 MINUTES OR LESS, GLUTEN-FREE, SOY-FREE, VEGETARIAN

This fast, spicy, sweet-roasted vegetable dish works best with a heavy cast iron griddle or oven-safe pan. The slight char that develops gives the beans a sweet, smoky flavor.

---

1 pound green beans, trimmed

2 tablespoons vegetable oil

2 tablespoons crushed and chopped fresh ginger

4 garlic cloves, crushed and chopped

2 tablespoons sugar

1 tablespoon red pepper flakes

1 tablespoon rice wine

1 teaspoon ground Sichuan peppercorns

1 teaspoon hot sesame oil

1 teaspoon kosher salt

1 teaspoon freshly ground white or black pepper

1. Place a large cast iron skillet or oven-safe pan 2 to 3 inches under the broiler element, set the broiler to high, and let the skillet heat for 5 minutes.

2. In a large bowl, toss the green beans with the vegetable oil, ginger, garlic, sugar, red pepper flakes, rice wine, peppercorns, sesame oil, salt, and pepper until the green beans are evenly coated.

3. Spread the seasoned green beans in a single layer in the skillet and broil for 2 to 4 minutes, until the green beans are blistered and lightly charred.

4. Serve immediately.

HEAT CHECK: Use more or less hot sesame oil and red pepper flakes to regulate the heat.

Vegetarian Mapo Tofu

SERVES 2 TO 4 / PREP TIME: 10 MINUTES / COOK TIME: 10 MINUTES

30 MINUTES OR LESS, VEGETARIAN

The combination of the spicy-hot elements and the numbing effect of the Sichuan peppercorns makes eating this dish with a good helping of rice almost mandatory.

---

2 tablespoons vegetable oil

1 pound firm or extra-firm tofu, diced into ½-inch pieces

2 tablespoons crushed and chopped fresh ginger

4 garlic cloves, crushed and chopped

4 ounces mushrooms, diced into ¼-inch pieces

3 tablespoons Lee Kum Kee Spicy Bean Sauce

1 tablespoon ground Sichuan peppercorns

1 tablespoon rice wine

1 teaspoon hot sesame oil

1 tablespoon soy sauce

1 bunch (6 to 8) scallions, cut into ¼-inch pieces

Steamed rice (see page 12), for serving

1. In a wok or large cast iron skillet, heat the vegetable oil over high heat until it shimmers. Add the tofu and stir-fry for 2 minutes.

2. Add the ginger and garlic and stir-fry for about 1 minute, until lightly browned. Add the mushrooms and stir-fry for 1 minute.

3. In a medium bowl, whisk together the bean sauce, peppercorns, rice wine, sesame oil, and soy sauce. Add the sauce to the wok and cook, stirring, for 2 minutes, until well incorporated.

4. Lower the heat to medium and gently stir in the scallions. Cook, covered, for 1 minute.

5. Serve over steamed rice.

HEAT CHECK: Use more or less bean sauce, red pepper flakes, and hot sesame oil to regulate the heat.

Bok Choy with Crispy Tofu

SERVES 2 TO 4 / PREP TIME: 10 MINUTES / COOK TIME: 20 MINUTES

30 MINUTES OR LESS, VEGETARIAN

For this simple Cantonese stir-fry, it's important to drain as much liquid from the tofu as possible to ensure its crispiness.

---

1 pound extra-firm tofu, drained and cut into ½-inch cubes

3 tablespoons cornstarch

1 teaspoon kosher salt

2 tablespoons vegetable oil

2 tablespoons crushed and chopped fresh ginger

3 garlic cloves, crushed and chopped

2 cups sliced bok choy (about 1-inch pieces)

1 bunch (6 to 8) scallions, cut into ½-pieces

2 tablespoons soy sauce

2 tablespoons ketchup

Steamed rice (see page 12), for serving

1. Seal the tofu, cornstarch, and salt in a large zip-top bag. Shake to coat evenly.

2. In a wok or large cast iron skillet, heat the oil for about 2 minutes, until it shimmers.

3. Add the coated tofu, ginger, and garlic and stir-fry for 5 minutes, or until the tofu is golden brown.

4. Remove and discard all but 2 tablespoons of oil.

5. Add the bok choy and stir-fry for 1 minute. Add the scallions and stir-fry for 30 seconds.

6. In a small bowl, whisk together the soy sauce and ketchup. Add the sauce to the wok and cook, stirring, for 1 minute, until the tofu and bok choy are evenly coated.

7. Serve over steamed rice.

TROUBLESHOOTING: To properly drain the tofu, place it between two paper towel–lined plates. Place a 1- to 2-pound weight, such as a can or bowl of water, on the top plate to press the tofu. Let it drain for 5 minutes. For even firmer tofu, freeze it overnight after draining. More liquid will drain while it thaws.

General Tso's Tofu

SERVES 2 TO 4 / PREP TIME: 10 MINUTES / COOK TIME: 20 MINUTES

30 MINUTES OR LESS, VEGETARIAN

This is a vegetarian version of my General Tso's Chicken recipe (see page 48). Use firm or extra-firm tofu if you'd prefer more texture.

---

1 pound silken tofu, drained and cut into ½-inch cubes

¼ cup plus 1 tablespoon cornstarch, divided

1 teaspoon ground white pepper

½ cup vegetable oil

¼ cup honey

2 tablespoons hoisin sauce

3 garlic cloves, crushed and chopped

1 tablespoon crushed and chopped fresh ginger

2 hot chiles, cut into ¼-inch pieces

1 tablespoon rice vinegar

1 teaspoon ground Sichuan peppercorns

1 teaspoon sesame seeds

1 bunch (6 to 8) scallions, cut into ¼-inch pieces

Steamed rice (see page 12), for serving

1. Seal the tofu, ¼ cup of cornstarch, and white pepper in a large zip-top bag. Shake to coat evenly.

2. In a wok or large cast iron skillet, heat the oil over high heat until it shimmers. Add the coated tofu and stir-fry for 5 minutes, or until the tofu is golden brown. Transfer the tofu to a plate.

3. Remove and discard all but 2 tablespoons of oil from the pan.

4. In a medium bowl, whisk together the honey, hoisin sauce, garlic, ginger, chiles, vinegar, and peppercorns and the remaining 1 tablespoon of cornstarch. Add the sauce to the wok and cook, stirring, for about 2 minutes, until the sauce thickens.

5. Add the fried tofu, tossing to coat.

6. Garnish with the sesame seeds and scallions and serve over steamed rice.

HEAT CHECK: You can regulate the spiciness of this dish by adjusting the amount of white pepper and chiles.

Kung Pao Tofu

SERVES 2 TO 4 / PREP TIME: 10 MINUTES / COOK TIME: 10 MINUTES

30 MINUTES OR LESS, VEGETARIAN

This is the vegetarian version of the well-known dish with chicken. *Kung pao* literally means "palace guardian" and refers to the position of the general for whom it was created.

---

1 pound extra-firm tofu, cut into ½-inch cubes

2 tablespoons sugar

1 tablespoon soy sauce

1 teaspoon ground Sichuan peppercorns

4 tablespoons cornstarch, divided

2 tablespoons vegetable oil

3 tablespoons crushed and chopped fresh ginger

2 garlic cloves, crushed and chopped

2 tablespoons rice vinegar

1 tablespoon Guilin chili paste

1 tablespoon rice wine

1 teaspoon hot sesame oil

1 red bell pepper, diced into ½-inch pieces

½ cup peanuts

1 bunch (6 to 8) scallions, cut into ¼-inch pieces

Steamed rice (see page 12), for serving

1. Seal the tofu, sugar, soy sauce, peppercorns, and 3 tablespoons of cornstarch in a large zip-top bag. Shake to coat evenly.

2. In a wok or large cast iron skillet, heat the vegetable oil over high heat until it shimmers. Add the ginger and garlic and stir-fry for about 1 minute, until lightly browned.

3. Add the coated tofu and stir-fry for 5 minutes, or until the tofu is lightly browned.

4. Add the vinegar, chili paste, rice wine, sesame oil, bell pepper, and peanuts and stir-fry for 1 minute. Add the scallions and stir-fry for 1 minute. Add the remaining 1 tablespoon of cornstarch and stir for about 2 minutes, until a glaze forms.

5. Serve over steamed rice.

SUBSTITUTION TIP: In a pinch, substitute the chili paste with a mixture of equal parts sriracha and soy sauce.

Buddha's Delight

This well-known dish has many variations, but it's always vegetarian. Elaborate recipes call for 10 or more different vegetables in a soy-flavored sauce.

¼ cup vegetable oil

1 pound extra-firm tofu, cut into ½-inch cubes

3 tablespoons crushed and chopped fresh ginger

5 garlic cloves, crushed and chopped

1 small carrot, roll cut into ½-inch pieces

1 small onion, diced into ½-inch pieces

1 red bell pepper, diced into ½-inch pieces

1 green bell pepper, diced into ½-inch pieces

4 ounces mushrooms, sliced

12 snow or sugar snap pea pods

¼ cup ketchup

2 tablespoons soy sauce

2 tablespoons rice wine

1 tablespoon Chinese five-spice powder

1 tablespoon cornstarch

1 bunch (6 to 8) scallions, cut diagonally into ½-inch pieces

Steamed rice (see page 12), for serving

1. In a wok or large cast iron skillet, heat the oil over high heat until it shimmers. Add the tofu and stir-fry for 3 to 4 minutes, or until the tofu is golden brown.

2. Add the ginger and garlic and stir-fry for 1 minute. Add the carrot and stir-fry for 1 minute. Add the onion and stir-fry for 1 minute. Add the red and green bell peppers and stir-fry for 1 minute. Add the mushrooms and stir-fry for 1 minute. Add the pea pods and stir-fry for 1 minute.

3. In a medium bowl, whisk together the ketchup, soy sauce, rice wine, five-spice powder, and cornstarch. Add the sauce and scallions to the wok and cook, stirring, for about 2 minutes, until a glaze forms.

4. Serve over steamed rice.

TROUBLESHOOTING: Roll cut carrots by slicing a whole carrot into ½-inch pieces at a 45-degree angle and rolling it a quarter of a turn after each successive cut. The uniform pieces will have multiple cooking surfaces that stir-fry faster than disks.

Egg Foo Young

SERVES 2 TO 4 / PREP TIME: 10 MINUTES / COOK TIME: 5 MINUTES

30 MINUTES OR LESS

This Chinese omelet was invented in the United States during the 1849 California gold rush to feed hungry Chinese and American laborers.

---

8 large eggs

1 teaspoon garlic salt

1 medium onion, diced into ¼-inch pieces

1 red or green bell pepper, diced into ¼-inch pieces

2 ounces mushrooms, diced into ¼-inch pieces

1 bunch (6 to 8) scallions, cut into ¼-inch pieces

6 teaspoons toasted sesame oil, divided

1 cup vegetable, chicken, beef, or pork broth

2 tablespoons soy sauce

2 tablespoons rice wine

2 tablespoons cornstarch

Steamed rice (see page 12), for serving

1. In a medium bowl, whisk together the eggs, garlic salt, onion, bell pepper, mushrooms, and scallions.

2. In a skillet or omelet pan, heat 1 teaspoon of the sesame oil over medium heat. Add ½ cup of the egg mixture to the skillet and fry for 2 to 3 minutes on each side. Repeat this process with the remaining 5 teaspoons of sesame oil and the egg mixture.

3. To make the gravy, in a small pot over medium heat, whisk together the broth, soy sauce, rice wine, and cornstarch. Bring to a simmer, stirring, for 2 minutes, until thickened.

4. Serve over steamed rice and top with the gravy.

Savory Egg Custard

SERVES 2 TO 4 / PREP TIME: 5 MINUTES / COOK TIME: 20 MINUTES

30 MINUTES OR LESS

This is a great side dish that can be prepared quickly for a tasty breakfast. And yes, for this preparation, the ramekins can sit directly in the water!

---

4 large eggs, beaten well

1 cup chicken broth, warm

½ teaspoon kosher salt

2 tablespoons soy sauce

1 tablespoon toasted sesame oil

2 scallions, minced

1. In a medium bowl, whisk together the eggs, broth, and salt until smooth.

2. Pour the mixture through a strainer into individual ramekins.

3. In a Dutch oven or deep pot over high heat, bring ¼ inch of water to a boil. Place the ramekins directly in the water. Cover the pot with a towel, add the lid, reduce the heat to low, and steam for 10 to 15 minutes, until the egg mixture turns to custard.

4. Uncover and let the ramekins cool in the pot for 5 minutes.

5. Garnish with the soy sauce, sesame oil, and scallions and serve.

TROUBLESHOOTING: The towel prevents condensation from getting in the custard. Alternatively, wrap each ramekin with plastic before adding them to the pot.

Smoky Tea Eggs

MAKES 6 SERVINGS / PREP TIME: 24 HOURS / COOK TIME: 10 MINUTES

VEGETARIAN

These tea eggs are a classic street food snack in China. The longer they soak in the spiced tea, the more flavor they absorb.

---

2 cups water

6 large eggs

½ cup soy sauce

2 tablespoons lapsang souchong leaves

2 tablespoons Chinese five-spice powder

1 tablespoon sugar

Kosher salt

Freshly ground black pepper

1. In a pot over medium-high heat, boil the water, eggs, soy sauce, lapsang souchong, five-spice powder, and sugar for 5 to 10 minutes, depending on how cooked you want the yolks (5 minutes for soft, 7 minutes for medium, and 10 minutes for hard).

2. Transfer the cooked eggs to a bowl of cold water to stop the cooking process. Remove the tea mixture from the heat and set aside until cool enough to handle (about room temperature).

3. Carefully tap on the egg shells, cracking them all over without removing the shells or breaking the egg apart.

4. Transfer the crackled eggs to a quart-size zip-top bag, then add the cooled tea mixture. Let the eggs marinate at room temperature overnight or for up to 24 hours.

5. Remove the eggs from the marinade, peel, and serve with salt and pepper.

SUBSTITUTION TIP: Use regular black tea and 1 tablespoon of smoked salt in place of the lapsang souchong.

COLD SPICY PEANUT
SESAME NOODLES,
PAGE 109

CHAPTER EIGHT

NOODLES AND FRIED RICE

In China, it's said there are rice people and noodle people. Some say that rice people come from Southern China, where people tend to be shorter and more muscular like grains of rice. Noodle people come from Northern China, and they are taller and thinner like noodles. This chapter proves that there's no need to choose.

Yang Chow Pork Fried Rice

SERVES 2 TO 4 / PREP TIME: 10 MINUTES / COOK TIME: 10 MINUTES

30 MINUTES OR LESS

On menus, this dish is often called "House Special Fried Rice" because of its multiple ingredients. In my version, I use cured Chinese sausage and shrimp.

---

2 tablespoons vegetable oil

2 large eggs, beaten

2 tablespoons crushed and chopped fresh ginger

3 garlic cloves, crushed and chopped

½ teaspoon kosher salt

2 cured Chinese sausages, roll cut into ½-inch pieces

1 medium onion, diced into ½-inch pieces

¼ pound medium shrimp, shelled, deveined, and halved lengthwise

1 cup frozen peas, thawed

2 cups day-old cooked rice

1 tablespoon soy sauce

1 teaspoon toasted sesame oil

½ teaspoon freshly ground black pepper

1. In a wok or large cast iron skillet, heat the vegetable oil over high heat until it shimmers.

2. In a medium bowl, whisk together the eggs, ginger, garlic, and salt. Pour the egg mixture into the wok and scramble for about 1 minute, until dry and firm. Transfer the scrambled eggs to a bowl.

3. Add the sausage to the wok and stir-fry for 1 minute. Add the onion and stir-fry for 1 minute. Add the shrimp and stir-fry for 1 minute.

4. Add the scrambled eggs and mix well for about 30 seconds. Add the peas and stir-fry for 1 minute. Add the rice, soy sauce, sesame oil, and black pepper and stir-fry for 1 minute, mixing well.

5. Serve immediately.

TROUBLESHOOTING: The key to making good fried rice is using leftover rice. Fresh rice overcooks and becomes soggy and sticky. In a pinch, spread out fresh rice on a pan and cool it in the refrigerator before using.

Sichuan Shrimp Fried Rice

SERVES 2 TO 4 / PREP TIME: 10 MINUTES / COOK TIME: 10 MINUTES

30 MINUTES OR LESS

Here's a classic spicy fried rice recipe. The heat of the hot sesame oil and red pepper flakes is enhanced by the tingling of the ground Sichuan peppercorns.

---

3 tablespoons vegetable oil, divided

2 large eggs, beaten

2 tablespoons crushed and chopped fresh ginger

3 garlic cloves, crushed and chopped

½ teaspoon kosher salt

1 medium onion, diced into ½-inch pieces

½ pound medium shrimp, peeled, deveined, and halved lengthwise

1 cup frozen peas, thawed

2 cups day-old cooked rice (see Troubleshooting on page 104)

1 teaspoon hot sesame oil

1 teaspoon red pepper flakes

1 teaspoon ground Sichuan peppercorns

1 tablespoon soy sauce

1 bunch (6 to 8) scallions, cut into ½-inch pieces

1. In a wok or large cast iron skillet, heat 2 tablespoons of vegetable oil over high heat until it shimmers.

2. In a medium bowl, whisk together the eggs, ginger, garlic, and salt. Pour the egg mixture into the wok and scramble for about 1 minute, until dry and firm. Transfer the scrambled eggs to a bowl.

3. Add the remaining 1 tablespoon of oil to the wok and heat for 1 minute, or until it shimmers. Add the onion and stir-fry for 1 minute. Add the shrimp and stir-fry for 1 minute. Add the peas and stir-fry for 1 minute. Add the rice and stir-fry for 1 minute.

4. Add the scrambled eggs, sesame oil, red pepper flakes, Sichuan peppercorns, and soy sauce and stir-fry for 1 minute.

5. Garnish with the scallions and serve immediately.

HEAT CHECK: You can regulate the spiciness of this dish by adjusting the amount of hot sesame oil and red pepper flakes.

Hunan Fried Rice

SERVES 2 TO 4 / PREP TIME: 10 MINUTES / COOK TIME: 20 MINUTES

30 MINUTES OR LESS, VEGETARIAN

This is a vegetarian recipe that replaces eggs and meat with tofu.

---

3 tablespoons vegetable oil, divided

1 pound extra-firm tofu, drained and crumbled

2 tablespoons crushed and chopped fresh ginger

3 garlic cloves, crushed and chopped

½ teaspoon kosher salt

1 medium onion, diced into ½-inch pieces

1 or 2 fresh hot chiles, minced

1 cup frozen peas, thawed

2 cups day-old cooked rice (see Troubleshooting on page 104)

1 teaspoon hot sesame oil

1 teaspoon ground Sichuan peppercorns

1 tablespoon soy sauce

1 bunch (6 to 8) scallions, cut into ½-inch pieces

1. In a wok or large cast iron skillet, heat 2 tablespoons of vegetable oil over high heat until it shimmers.

2. Add the tofu, ginger, garlic, and salt and stir-fry for 3 to 4 minutes, or until the tofu is lightly browned.

3. Add the remaining 1 tablespoon of vegetable oil to the wok and heat for 1 minute, or until it shimmers. Add the onion and stir-fry for 1 minute. Add the chiles and stir-fry for 1 minute. Add the peas and stir-fry for 1 minute. Add the rice and stir-fry for 1 minute.

4. Add the sesame oil, peppercorns, and soy sauce and stir-fry for 1 minute.

5. Garnish with the scallions and serve immediately.

HEAT CHECK: Substitute toasted sesame oil for the hot sesame oil and leave out the minced chiles for a milder version.

Lapsang Souchong Pork Fried Rice

SERVES 2 TO 4 / PREP TIME: 10 MINUTES / COOK TIME: 10 MINUTES

30 MINUTES OR LESS

Using lapsang souchong to cook the rice adds a smoky flavor. It's said the tea was discovered accidentally when farmers tried to speed up the drying process over pine fires. The smoked tea sold faster than regular tea!

4 tablespoons vegetable oil, divided

2 large eggs, beaten

½ teaspoon kosher salt

2 tablespoons crushed and chopped fresh ginger

3 garlic cloves, crushed and chopped

½ pound ground pork

1 medium onion, diced into ½-inch pieces

1 cup frozen peas, thawed

2 cups day-old lapsang souchong rice (see Troubleshooting on page 104)

1 tablespoon soy sauce

1 teaspoon toasted or hot sesame oil

1 bunch (6 to 8) scallions, cut into ½-inch pieces

1. In a wok or large cast iron skillet, heat 2 tablespoons of vegetable oil over high heat until it shimmers.

2. In a medium bowl, whisk together the eggs and salt. Pour the egg mixture into the wok and scramble for about 1 minute, until dry and firm. Transfer the scrambled eggs to a bowl.

3. Add the remaining 2 tablespoons of vegetable oil to the wok and heat for 1 minute or until it shimmers.

4. Add the ginger, garlic, and pork and stir-fry for 2 minutes. Add the onion and stir-fry for 1 minute. Add the peas and stir-fry for 1 minute.

5. Add the rice, scrambled eggs, soy sauce, sesame oil, and scallions and stir-fry for 1 minute.

6. Serve immediately.

TROUBLESHOOTING: Follow the rice cooking method on page 12, using 1 cup of long-grain white rice and 2 cups of tea instead of water. This makes 2 cups of cooked rice.

Scallion Pancakes

SERVES 2 TO 4 / PREP TIME: 10 MINUTES / COOK TIME: 10 MINUTES

30 MINUTES OR LESS, GLUTEN-FREE, SOY-FREE

This quick and savory Chinese flatbread can be eaten alone, dipped in a sauce, or used as a wrap for stir-fries.

---

1 cup chopped scallions

¾ cup self-rising flour

¾ cup warm water

1 large egg

1 tablespoon crushed and chopped
   fresh ginger

2 garlic cloves, crushed and chopped

1 teaspoon toasted or hot sesame oil

½ teaspoon kosher salt

4 teaspoons vegetable oil, divided

1. In a medium bowl, mix together the scallions, flour, water, egg, ginger, garlic, sesame oil, and salt for 2 minutes, or until smooth.

2. In a skillet, heat 2 teaspoons of vegetable oil over medium-high heat for 1 minute or until it shimmers.

3. Pour in enough batter to make a 6-inch pancake. Fry on each side for about 1 minute, or until golden brown. Transfer the pancake to a plate. Repeat this process with the remaining batter and 2 tablespoons of vegetable oil. It should make 4 to 6 pancakes.

4. Serve warm.

Cold Spicy Peanut Sesame Noodles

SERVES 2 TO 4 / PREP TIME: 10 MINUTES / COOK TIME: 20 MINUTES

30 MINUTES OR LESS, SOY-FREE, VEGETARIAN

There are several layers of flavor and texture in this dish: cool and sweet, then nutty, then crunchy, then hot-spicy. And that's just the first bite!

¼ cup creamy peanut butter

2 tablespoons toasted sesame oil

2 tablespoons honey, maple syrup, or corn syrup

1 teaspoon hot sesame oil

8 ounces pasta, cooked to al dente, rinsed in cold water, and drained

1 red bell pepper, diced into ¼-inch pieces

1 bunch (6 to 8) scallions, cut into ¼-inch pieces

1 tablespoon sesame seeds

1. In a large bowl, whisk together the peanut butter, toasted sesame oil, honey, and hot sesame oil for 1 minute, or until smooth.

2. Add the pasta and toss for 1 minute, or until the pasta is evenly coated.

3. Add the bell pepper and scallions and toss for 30 seconds.

4. Garnish with the sesame seeds and serve cold.

SUBSTITUTION TIP: Replace peanut butter with tahini, a sesame-based butter.

Crispy Chicken Chow Mein

SERVES 2 TO 4 / PREP TIME: 10 MINUTES / COOK TIME: 10 MINUTES

30 MINUTES OR LESS

Chow mein means "fried noodles" in Chinese. The fried noodles are crispy, almost deep-fried in the oil.

---

8 ounces Chinese noodles or linguine, cooked to al dente and drained

2 tablespoons vegetable oil

2 tablespoons crushed and chopped fresh ginger

3 garlic cloves, crushed and chopped

1 pound boneless chicken thighs, cut into ½-inch pieces

1 medium onion, diced into ½-inch pieces

1 red bell pepper, diced into ½-inch pieces

1 bunch (6 to 8) scallions, cut into ½-inch pieces

¼ cup oyster sauce

¼ cup ketchup

2 tablespoons rice wine

1. Seal the noodles and oil in a large zip-top bag. Shake for 1 minute, until the noodles are lightly coated.

2. In a wok or large cast iron skillet over medium heat, stir-fry the coated noodles and oil from the bag for 2 minutes, or until the noodles are lightly browned and crispy. Transfer the noodles to a plate or shallow bowl, leaving the remaining oil in the wok.

3. Add the ginger and garlic and stir-fry for about 1 minute, until lightly browned.

4. Add the chicken and stir-fry for 2 minutes. Add the onion and stir-fry for 1 minute. Add the bell pepper and stir-fry for 1 minute.

5. Add the scallions, oyster sauce, ketchup, and rice wine and stir-fry for 1 minute.

6. Pour everything over the crispy noodles and serve.

TROUBLESHOOTING: Instead of frying, bake the oil-tossed noodles in a shallow oven-safe pan in a 400°F oven for 10 minutes, or until lightly browned and crispy.

Mu Shu Pork

SERVES 2 TO 4 / PREP TIME: 10 MINUTES / COOK TIME: 10 MINUTES

30 MINUTES OR LESS

Although this dish is served with thin Mandarin pancakes here in the United States, in China, it's often served over rice or noodles.

---

1 ounce tree ear mushrooms

1 pound pork loin, sliced across the grain into ¼-inch strips

½ cup hoisin sauce, divided

1 tablespoon soy sauce

2 tablespoons rice wine

1 teaspoon hot sesame oil

4 tablespoons vegetable oil, divided

2 large eggs, beaten

1 teaspoon kosher salt

½ teaspoon ground white pepper

2 tablespoons crushed and chopped fresh ginger

3 garlic cloves, crushed and chopped

2 cups Napa cabbage, cut into ¼-inch pieces

1 bunch (6 to 8) scallions, cut into ¼-inch pieces

6 to 8 flour tortillas

1. Soak the mushrooms in boiled hot water for 15 minutes, then drain and slice.

2. Seal the sliced pork, ¼ cup of hoisin sauce, the soy sauce, rice wine, and sesame oil in a large zip-top bag. Massage for 1 minute and let marinate until ready to use.

3. In a wok or large cast iron skillet, heat 2 tablespoons of vegetable oil over high heat until it shimmers.

4. In a medium bowl, whisk together the eggs, salt, and pepper. Pour the egg mixture into the wok and scramble for about 1 minute, until dry and firm. Transfer the scrambled eggs to a bowl.

5. In the wok, heat the remaining 2 tablespoons of vegetable oil for 1 minute until it shimmers. Add the ginger and garlic and stir-fry for about 1 minute, until lightly browned.

6. Add the marinated pork and scrambled eggs and stir-fry for 1 minute. Add the sliced mushrooms and stir-fry for 1 minute. Add the cabbage and stir-fry for 1 minute. Add the scallions and stir-fry for 1 minute.

continued

Mu Shu Pork *continued*

7. Spread the remaining ¼ cup of hoisin sauce on one side of each tortilla. Add the stir-fry, fold, and serve.

SUBSTITUTION TIP: Replace store-bought flour tortillas with homemade tortillas using my Dumpling Wrappers recipe (see page 19). Roll out the dough to make 6-inch circles and lightly brown them in a dry skillet over medium-low heat.

Shrimp Lo Mein

SERVES 2 TO 4 / PREP TIME: 10 MINUTES / COOK TIME: 20 MINUTES

30 MINUTES OR LESS

Lo mein literally means "stirred noodles," and they are softer than chow mein noodles. They are boiled, drained, and either mixed in after the ingredients and sauce are stir-fried or served under the ingredients and sauce.

---

2 tablespoons vegetable oil

2 tablespoons crushed and chopped fresh ginger

3 garlic cloves, crushed and chopped

1 medium onion, diced into ½-inch pieces

1 pound medium shrimp, shelled, deveined, and halved lengthwise

1 red bell pepper, diced into ½-inch pieces

1 bunch (6 to 8) scallions, cut into ½ pieces

¼ cup oyster sauce

¼ cup ketchup

2 tablespoons soy sauce

2 tablespoons rice wine

8 ounces Chinese noodles or linguine, cooked to al dente and drained

1. In a wok or large cast iron skillet, heat the vegetable oil over high heat until it shimmers. Add the ginger and garlic and stir-fry for about 1 minute, until lightly browned.

2. Add the onion and stir-fry for 1 minute. Add the shrimp and stir-fry for 1 minute. Add the bell pepper and stir-fry for 1 minute. Add the scallions and stir-fry for 1 minute.

3. Add the oyster sauce, ketchup, soy sauce, and rice wine and cook, stirring, for 1 minute.

4. Serve over the noodles.

SUBSTITUTION TIP: You can substitute other sliced meats, seafood, or extra-firm tofu for the shrimp.

Beef Chow Fun

SERVES 2 TO 4 / PREP TIME: 10 MINUTES / COOK TIME: 20 MINUTES

30 MINUTES OR LESS

This rice noodle dish is a classic Cantonese stir-fry with steak. The key here is to soak the noodles just long enough so they can be stir-fried and hold together.

---

2 quarts water

8 ounces wide rice noodles

1 pound sirloin strip steak, cut against the grain into ⅛-inch pieces

2 tablespoons soy sauce

1 tablespoon cornstarch

2 tablespoons vegetable oil

2 tablespoons crushed and chopped fresh ginger

3 garlic cloves, crushed and chopped

1 cup fresh bean sprouts

2 tablespoons rice wine

1 teaspoon toasted or hot sesame oil

1 teaspoon sugar

1 bunch (6 to 8) scallions, cut into ½-inch pieces

1. In a wok or soup pot over high heat, bring the water to a boil. Remove the wok from the heat and place the noodles in the hot water to soak for 6 to 10 minutes, until al dente. Drain the noodles and set aside.

2. Seal the steak, soy sauce, and cornstarch in a large zip-top bag. Massage for 2 minutes.

3. In a wok or large cast iron skillet, heat the vegetable oil over high heat until it shimmers. Add the ginger and garlic and stir-fry for about 1 minute, until lightly browned.

4. Add the marinated steak and stir-fry for 1 minute for medium rare or 2 minutes for medium. Add the bean sprouts and stir-fry for 1 minute.

5. Add the rice wine, sesame oil, and sugar and cook, stirring, for 1 minute. Add the drained noodles and toss and stir-fry for 1 minute. Add the scallions and stir-fry for 1 minute.

6. Serve immediately.

TROUBLESHOOTING: The "grain" of meat is the direction of the muscle fibers. Cutting across it results in more tender pieces.

Pork Mei Fun

SERVES 2 TO 4 / PREP TIME: 10 MINUTES / COOK TIME: 10 MINUTES

Mei fun noodles are thin rice noodles that require very little time to soften in warm water. They are sometimes labeled "Thai rice noodles."

8 ounces thin rice noodles

1 pound pork loin, cut across the grain into ¼-inch strips

1 tablespoon cornstarch

1 teaspoon ground white pepper

2 tablespoons vegetable oil

2 tablespoons crushed and chopped fresh ginger

3 garlic cloves, crushed and chopped

1 medium carrot, cut into matchsticks

1 medium onion, halved and cut into ¼-inch strips

1 cup shredded cabbage (about ¼ inch wide)

¼ cup oyster sauce

2 tablespoons soy sauce

1 tablespoon rice wine

1. Fill a medium bowl with hot tap water. Add the noodles and soak for 6 to 10 minutes, until al dente. Drain the noodles and set aside.

2. Seal the pork, cornstarch, and white pepper in a large zip-top bag. Massage for 2 minutes.

3. In a wok or large cast iron skillet, heat the oil over high heat until it shimmers. Add the ginger and garlic and stir-fry for about 1 minute, until lightly browned.

4. Add the carrot and stir-fry for 1 minute. Add the onion and stir-fry for 1 minute. Add the marinated pork and stir-fry for 2 minutes. Add the cabbage and stir-fry for 1 minute.

5. Add the oyster sauce, soy sauce, and rice wine and cook, stirring, for 1 minute.

6. Add the drained noodles and toss and stir-fry for 1 minute, until well combined.

7. Serve immediately.

Sticky Rice in Lotus Leaves
(Lo Mai Gai)

SERVES 2 TO 4 / PREP TIME: 15 MINUTES / COOK TIME: 40 MINUTES

This is a classic Southern Chinese dim sum dish. The aroma is wonderful when you unwrap the steaming lotus leaf packet.

---

4 to 5 dried lotus leaves

2 cured Chinese sausages, roll cut into ¼-inch pieces

2 cups water

1 cup sweet glutinous rice

1 tablespoon soy sauce

1 tablespoon sugar

1 teaspoon toasted sesame oil

1 teaspoon Chinese five-spice powder

2 tablespoons vegetable oil

2 tablespoons crushed and chopped fresh ginger

3 garlic cloves, crushed and chopped

½ pound boneless chicken thighs, cut into ½-inch cubes

½ cup diced mushrooms (¼-inch pieces)

2 tablespoons oyster sauce

½ cup honey-roasted peanuts

1. Fill the sink or a large pan with water. Add the lotus leaves and soak for 15 minutes, weighing them down with a plate if needed. Drain them and set aside.

2. In a 2-quart saucepan with a lid, combine the sausage, water, rice, soy sauce, sugar, sesame oil, and five-spice powder. Bring to a boil over high heat.

3. Immediately turn the heat to low. Cook the rice for 15 minutes without lifting the lid, then remove from the heat and uncover. Stir to evenly distribute the sausage.

4. In a wok or large cast iron skillet, heat the vegetable oil over high heat until it shimmers. Add the ginger and garlic and stir-fry for about 1 minute, until lightly browned.

5. Add the chicken and stir-fry for 1 minute. Add the mushrooms and stir-fry for 1 minute. Add the oyster sauce and peanuts and stir-fry for 1 minute.

6. Place 3 tablespoons of cooked rice and sausage in the center of each lotus leaf. Place 1 tablespoon of chicken and mushrooms in the center of the rice and sausage. Place another 3 tablespoons of rice and sausage on top of the chicken and mushrooms.

7. Wrap the lotus leaf around the filling as you would a burrito and tie it with string.

8. Place a wok or pot fitted with a steamer basket over high heat. Add enough water to come up 1 inch from the bottom of the basket. When the water boils, immediately place the packets in the basket, cover, and steam for 15 minutes.

9. Serve immediately.

TAKE A SHORTCUT: If you're eating immediately, don't bother tying the packets. Just tuck the loose ends underneath. Refrigerate or freeze tied packets for later. Steam them for 10 minutes if refrigerated or 20 minutes if frozen.

SPICY SESAME SOY DIPPING SAUCE, PAGE 122

CHAPTER NINE

SAUCES AND CONDIMENTS

As in most culinary traditions, Chinese sauces were developed to help preserve and flavor foods before there was refrigeration. Salty soy, spicy pepper, sweet honey, and pungent vinegar all have antibacterial and preservative characteristics. This chapter mixes and matches these ingredients to create new flavors in marinades, rubs, and condiments.

Soy and Ketchup Dipping Sauce

MAKES ¾ CUP / PREP TIME: 2 MINUTES

30 MINUTES OR LESS, VEGETARIAN

My favorite explanation for the Chinese origin of ketchup is that when early Chinese immigrants wanted gravy with their stir-fries, they said "get jup." *Jup* is the Cantonese word for a fermented fish sauce. Use this dip for my Boiled Dumplings (*Jiaozi*, see page 18) or as a marinade for my Cast Iron Roasted Chinese Chicken Thighs (see page 45).

½ cup ketchup

¼ cup soy sauce

1 tablespoon toasted or hot sesame oil

1. In a small bowl, whisk together the ketchup, soy sauce, and sesame oil until well combined.

2. Use right away or store in an airtight container in the refrigerator for about 1 week.

Soy and Vinegar Dipping Sauce

MAKES ¼ CUP / PREP TIME: 2 MINUTES

30 MINUTES OR LESS, VEGETARIAN

This simple dipping sauce has salty, sweet, and sour flavors. Experiment with the proportions of the salty soy sauce and the sour-sweetness of the vinegar. Use this as a marinade, stir-fry sauce, or dipping sauce.

¼ cup soy sauce

2 tablespoons balsamic vinegar glaze

1. In a small bowl, whisk together the soy sauce and balsamic vinegar glaze until well combined.

2. Use right away or store in an airtight container at room temperature or in the refrigerator for about 1 week.

SUBSTITUTION TIP: Experiment with the balsamic glaze, which comes in many flavors, such as chili, plum, and wine.

Spicy Sesame Soy Dipping Sauce

MAKES ¼ CUP / PREP TIME: 2 MINUTES

30 MINUTES OR LESS, VEGETARIAN

This works as either a dip or a glaze for roasting meats. It goes especially well with deep-fried appetizers like my Egg Rolls (see page 24) and Spring Rolls (see page 26).

¼ cup soy sauce

1 tablespoon honey or maple syrup

1 teaspoon hot sesame oil

1. In a small bowl, whisk together the soy sauce, honey, and sesame oil until well combined.

2. Use right away or store in an airtight container in the refrigerator for about 1 week.

SUBSTITUTION TIP: Brown sugar can be substituted for the honey or maple syrup.

Sweet and Sour Duck Sauce

MAKES 29 OUNCES / PREP TIME: 10 MINUTES

30 MINUTES OR LESS, GLUTEN-FREE, SOY-FREE, VEGETARIAN

There's no duck in this sauce, but it was traditionally used as a condiment when serving roasted duck. It's also great as a dipping sauce for my Sweet and Sour Spareribs (see page 31) and Sweet and Sour Chicken Wings (see page 29).

1 (20-ounce) jar applesauce

1 (8-ounce) can crushed pineapple

3 tablespoons balsamic vinegar glaze

1. In a medium bowl, whisk together the applesauce, pineapple, and balsamic vinegar glaze until well combined.

2. Use right away or store in an airtight container in the refrigerator for about 1 week.

HEAT CHECK: Add 1 teaspoon of hot sesame oil or sriracha for a little heat.

Hot Mustard Sauce

MAKES ¼ CUP / PREP TIME: 10 MINUTES

30 MINUTES OR LESS, GLUTEN-FREE, SOY-FREE, VEGETARIAN

This a dip for those who really like it hot. The vinegar takes the heat of the mustard up into the sinuses to clear your head.

---

3 tablespoons rice vinegar   2 tablespoons ground yellow mustard

1. In a small bowl, whisk together the vinegar and mustard and let it sit for 5 minutes. As needed, add more vinegar or mustard, a little at a time, for desired thickness.

2. Use right away or store in an airtight container in the refrigerator.

HEAT CHECK: Not hot enough for you? Add 1 teaspoon of hot sesame oil. Another option: Combine 1 teaspoon of this sauce with ½ cup of my Sweet and Sour Duck Sauce (see page 123) for an interesting twist.

Vegetarian Oyster Sauce

MAKES 1 CUP / PREP TIME: 10 MINUTES

30 MINUTES OR LESS, VEGETARIAN

This is a good substitute for real oyster sauce, especially if you or someone you're serving has seafood allergies or if you want a vegetarian or vegan recipe.

4 ounces mushrooms, crushed and chopped or puréed

½ cup ketchup

¼ cup soy sauce

1 teaspoon Chinese five-spice powder

1 teaspoon toasted sesame oil

1. In a medium bowl, whisk together the mushrooms, ketchup, soy sauce, five-spice powder, and sesame oil until well combined.

2. Use right away or store in an airtight container in the refrigerator for about 1 week.

SUBSTITUTION TIP: Instead of fresh mushrooms, use 1 tablespoon of dried mushroom powder, which is available online. Make your own powder by grinding dried mushrooms in a food processor or blender.

FIVE-SPICE POACHED PEARS IN WINE, PAGE 128

CHAPTER TEN

DESSERTS

Chinese diners enjoy sweet desserts, but they aren't always present en force on Chinese American restaurant menus. This may be because these restaurants first catered to busy workers who couldn't linger for dessert. Regardless, give these desserts a try and linger all you want!

Five-Spice Poached Pears in Wine

SERVES 2 TO 4 / PREP TIME: 10 MINUTES / COOK TIME: 1 HOUR

GLUTEN-FREE, SOY-FREE, VEGETARIAN

Make this dessert in advance and serve it warm, at room temperature, or refrigerated. If using unripe pears, poach them a little longer.

---

3 ripe pears, cored and sliced into
  24 wedges

1 bottle fruit-flavored dessert wine

3 tablespoons crushed and chopped
  fresh ginger

1 tablespoon Chinese five-spice powder

1. In a shallow pan, place the pears, dessert wine, ginger, and five-spice powder. Add more wine or water to just cover the pears.

2. Bring to a simmer over medium heat and cook the pears for about 30 minutes, turning them once, until the liquid is reduced by half and the pears are easily pierced with a fork.

3. Transfer the pears to a covered bowl and refrigerate.

4. Reduce the sauce by half again, over medium heat, for about 30 minutes. Remove from the heat and let cool, depending on the desired temperature for serving.

5. Serve the pears with cold or room temperature syrup.

SUBSTITUTION TIP: Any sweet wine can be used instead of dessert wine. Another good option is ice wine, which is a sweet wine made from grapes that have been frozen on the vine.

Amaretto Cream with Mandarin Oranges

SERVES 2 TO 4 / PREP TIME: 15 MINUTES / COOK TIME: 1 HOUR 30 MINUTES

GLUTEN-FREE, SOY-FREE

Think of this as almond-flavored Jell-O for adults. It's known as almond tofu in China, though there is no tofu in it.

---

4 cups half-and-half, divided

½ cup sugar

¼ cup amaretto

3 packets Knox unflavored gelatin

1 (15-ounce can) mandarin oranges, drained

1. In a 2-quart saucepan over medium heat, bring 3 cups of half-and-half, the sugar, and the amaretto to a simmer.

2. In a medium bowl, whisk the gelatin into the remaining 1 cup of half-and-half until smooth.

3. Stirring constantly, pour the gelatin mixture into the simmering saucepan and cook for 2 minutes, or until smooth.

4. Pour the mixture into individual dessert bowls or a shallow baking dish. Place in the refrigerator or freezer to cool and set, depending on how soon dessert will be served.

5. When jelled, if using a single shallow baking dish, use a butter knife or spatula to cut the custard into 1-inch blocks and place several of them into dessert dishes, then add the oranges and serve. If using individual dessert bowls, add some oranges to each bowl and serve.

SUBSTITUTION TIP: Try other liquors or extracts instead of amaretto. Orange, coffee, coconut, and chocolate liqueurs are all favorites of mine!

Sweet Egg Custard Dessert

SERVES 2 TO 4 / PREP TIME: 5 MINUTES / COOK TIME: 20 MINUTES

30 MINUTES OR LESS, GLUTEN-FREE, SOY-FREE

Some say the smooth, silky texture of this dessert will calm your nerves and enhance your health and complexion. I just think it tastes great!

---

1 cup whole milk

¼ cup sugar

1 teaspoon vanilla extract

3 large eggs, beaten

Ground cinnamon and sugar or mandarin oranges, for serving

1. In a medium bowl, whisk together the milk, sugar, and vanilla for 2 minutes, until the sugar is dissolved.

2. Add the eggs and whisk for 1 minute, until smooth.

3. In a Dutch oven or deep pot over high heat, bring ¼ inch of water to a boil. Fill ramekins by pouring the mixture through a strainer. Place the ramekins directly in the water. Cover the pot with a towel, add the lid, reduce the heat to low, and steam for 10 minutes, until the egg mixture turns to custard.

4. Remove from the heat, leaving the cover on, and let rest for 10 minutes.

5. Remove the cover and serve warm, garnished with cinnamon and sugar, or refrigerate for 1 to 2 hours before serving.

Pumpkin Pancakes

SERVES 2 TO 4 / PREP TIME: 10 MINUTES / COOK TIME: 10 MINUTES

30 MINUTES OR LESS, SOY-FREE, VEGETARIAN

This is a simple version of a sweet and savory dessert that originated in Southern China. The use of oil for shallow frying makes them puffy with a chewy, crisp exterior.

---

1 cup pumpkin pie filling

½ cup self-rising flour

¼ cup sugar

1 tablespoon toasted sesame oil

1 teaspoon Chinese five-spice powder

½ cup vegetable oil

Powdered sugar, for serving

Ground cinnamon, for serving

1. Stir together the pumpkin, flour, sugar, sesame oil, and five-spice powder for 2 minutes, or until the batter is smooth.

2. In a large cast iron skillet, heat the vegetable oil over medium-high heat until it shimmers.

3. Drop 2 tablespoons of batter into the vegetable oil for each pancake. Fry each side for 30 to 40 seconds, or until golden brown on both sides.

4. Sprinkle the pancakes with powdered sugar and cinnamon and serve.

SUBSTITUTION TIP: Instead of cinnamon and sugar, try serving these with honey or maple syrup.

Home Takeout Menus

Here are some suggested menus from recipes in this book. Have fun creating your own favorites!

DIY DIM SUM

Dim sum was originally for people headed to or from work. It is traditionally served with tea, so try serving these family style with tea at home.

- **Pot Stickers** (*Guotie*, page 22)

- **Pork Spareribs with Black Bean Sauce** (see page 64)

- **Wonton Soup** (see page 36)

- **Egg Rolls** (see page 24)

- **Sticky Rice in Lotus Leaves** (*Lo Mai Gai*, see page 116)

CHINESE NEW YEAR FEAST

These dishes are symbolic. Hot and sour soup's many ingredients symbolize plenty. Dumplings and spring rolls represent wealth. Long noodles are said to ensure long life. Chicken symbolizes family togetherness. Whole fish brings prosperity and good luck and signifies good times with family and friends.

- **Hot and Sour Soup** (see page 39)

- **Boiled Dumplings** (*Jiaozi*, see page 18)

- **Spring Rolls** (see page 26)

- **Crispy Chicken Chow Mein** (see page 110)

- **Whole Fried Fish** (see page 82)

SICHUAN NIGHT

If you and your guests are always reaching for the hot sauce, you'll want to fill your table with these fiery dishes from China's Sichuan Province—chiles, hot sesame oil, and ground Sichuan peppercorns wake up your taste buds. The one exception is Chairman Mao's favorite, Red Cooked Pork.

- **Cold Spicy Peanut Sesame Noodles** (see page 109)

- **Sichuan Chicken** (see page 53)

- **Sichuan Beef and Vegetables** (see page 68)

- **General Tso's Chicken** (see page 48)

- **Red Cooked Pork** (*Hong Shao Rou*, see page 60)

CLASSIC CANTONESE TAKEOUT

This menu reminds me of some favorites from my Uncle Jimmy's restaurant takeout menu while I was growing up in suburban Boston in the 1970s.

- **Teriyaki Beef Skewers** (see page 32)
- **Egg Rolls** (see page 24)
- **Sweet and Sour Chicken Wings** (see page 29)
- **Yang Chow Pork Fried Rice** (see page 104)
- **Beef and Broccoli with Oyster Sauce** (see page 66)

VEGETARIAN AND VEGAN TAKEOUT

No animals were harmed in the creation of the following menu. Most recipes in this book can be adapted for vegetarians by replacing meat and fish with tofu and vegetables.

- **Cucumber Salad** (see page 40)
- **General Tso's Tofu** (see page 96)
- **Roasted Sichuan Eggplant and Green Beans** (see page 90)
- **Buddha's Delight** (see page 98)
- **Vegetarian Mapo Tofu** (see page 94)

MEASUREMENT CONVERSIONS

VOLUME EQUIVALENTS (LIQUID)

US STANDARD	US STANDARD (OUNCES)	METRIC (APPROXIMATE)
2 tablespoons	1 fl. oz.	30 mL
¼ cup	2 fl. oz.	60 mL
½ cup	4 fl. oz.	120 mL
1 cup	8 fl. oz.	240 mL
1½ cups	12 fl. oz.	355 mL
2 cups or 1 pint	16 fl. oz.	475 mL
4 cups or 1 quart	32 fl. oz.	1 L
1 gallon	128 fl. oz.	4 L

OVEN TEMPERATURES

FAHRENHEIT	CELSIUS (APPROXIMATE)
250°F	120°C
300°F	150°C
325°F	165°C
350°F	180°C
375°F	190°C
400°F	200°C
425°F	220°C
450°F	230°C

VOLUME EQUIVALENTS (DRY)

US STANDARD	METRIC (APPROXIMATE)
⅛ teaspoon	0.5 mL
¼ teaspoon	1 mL
½ teaspoon	2 mL
¾ teaspoon	4 mL
1 teaspoon	5 mL
1 tablespoon	15 mL
¼ cup	59 mL
⅓ cup	79 mL
½ cup	118 mL
⅔ cup	156 mL
¾ cup	177 mL
1 cup	235 mL
2 cups or 1 pint	475 mL
3 cups	700 mL
4 cups or 1 quart	1 L

WEIGHT EQUIVALENTS

US STANDARD	METRIC (APPROXIMATE)
½ ounce	15 g
1 ounce	30 g
2 ounces	60 g
4 ounces	115 g
8 ounces	225 g
12 ounces	340 g
16 ounces or 1 pound	455 g

Resources

Equipment

AMAZON

A good place to research and order specialty cooking equipment such as woks, cleavers, steamers, cutting boards, and other tools. *amazon.com*

EBAY

A good place to search for specialty equipment and supplies. *ebay.com*

WEBSTAURANTSTORE

A webstore based in Lancaster, Pennsylvania, that bills itself as the largest restaurant supply website and sells cooking supplies and equipment at wholesale prices. *webstaurantstore.com*

THE WOK SHOP

A store with a wide selection of Asian cooking equipment based in San Francisco's Chinatown. *wokshop.com*

Ingredients

AMAZON

A good place to research and order specialty Chinese ingredients such as dried spices, sauces, noodles, and mushrooms. *amazon.com*

MIMODIAN

A specialty online store for Chinese cooking ingredients that's also on Facebook and Instagram. *mimodian.com*

YAMIBUY

An online Asian marketplace started by a frustrated college student when he couldn't find authentic Chinese ingredients. *yamibuy.com*

Chinese Food Blogs

APPETITE FOR CHINA
A food blog by Diana Kuan, a Brooklyn, New York–based food writer and cooking teacher. *appetiteforchina.com*

CHINA SICHUAN FOOD
A food and cooking blog by Elaine Luo, a native of the Sichuan Province who shares her love of cooking and culture across China. *chinasichuanfood.com*

TOP CHINA TRAVEL
A travel site that provides a quick overview of Chinese food and culture through 5,000 years of China's history. *topchinatravel.com/china-guide /history-of-chinese-cuisine*

THE WOKS OF LIFE
A fun, interesting, and informative Chinese food blog by a Chinese American family based in the Northeastern United States. *thewoksoflife.com*

Index

Acknowledgments

THIS BOOK WAS made possible with lots of assistance and advice. Thank you to Joan, my wonderfully supportive, patient, and understanding wife. Your good-natured willingness to accept my request to "crack the whip" at the beginning of this process enabled me to get started. Your gentle insistence and perseverance pushed me on to finish this project. We both know that I'm way too easily distracted to have done this without your help. Thanks also for pausing your own activities to patiently listen while I sought your advice on my rambling prose. I love you, too.

Thanks also to Arturo Conde, my editor from Callisto Media, who somehow managed to keep me organized and on schedule. All of your editing suggestions and changes made my work better. I appreciated your positive and thoughtful collaboration from our initial conversations about the introduction to gathering and organizing the recipes. It was fun, challenging, enlightening, and a pleasure to work with you, Arturo.

Finally, thanks to Callisto Media for coming up with such an interesting and innovative way of publishing books. As someone who enjoys exploring possibilities and is intrigued by out-of-the-box thinking, your use of big data to reimagine publishing is fascinating.

About the Author

CHRIS TOY has been teaching Asian cooking for over 30 years. Adopted by Alfred and Grace Toy, a Chinese American couple, Chris moved to the United States from Hong Kong in 1958. He grew up near Boston, graduating from Quincy public schools, Bowdoin College, and Brown University, where he earned a master's degree in teaching. A retired teacher, principal, and international educational consultant, Chris learned Chinese cooking from his mother in his family's home and restaurant kitchens. As an adult, he has explored and become skilled at cooking up new Asian recipes that incorporate fresh local ingredients.

Chris started teaching Chinese cooking on weekends at a local kitchen store in Portland, Maine, to make some extra money, supplementing his first job teaching high school social studies. The combination of teaching and cooking immediately resonated with him. Today, in addition to teaching regularly at local kitchen stores, Chris teaches adult education classes in several communities around Bath, Maine, where he lives with his wife, Joan. Chris's popular hands-on classes are built around his teaching skills and deep appreciation for fresh, simply prepared food. Chris's cooking incorporates straightforward methods, fresh ingredients, and unique flavors, which all draw family and friends together to enjoy great food and company.

When not sharing his love of cooking, Chris, a registered Maine guide, enjoys hiking, biking, kayaking, and camping trips in the woods and waters of Maine's great outdoors. Of course, preparing and sharing good food is always a highlight of his excursions. You can find Chris online at *christoy.net*. Subscribe to his YouTube cooking channel at *youtube.com/user/cmtoy/videos*.

Printed in the USA
CPSIA information can be obtained
at www.ICGtesting.com
LVHW081657301123
764704LV00004B/62

9 781646 115877